Marc Zao-Sanders is the co-founder and the CEO of filtered.com, a learning tech company that focuses on developing business skills within the workplace and using data to identify, analyse and deliver the most important skills to organization members. Marc Zao-Sanders began his career in strategy and now regularly writes about topics including algorithms, learning and productivity in *Harvard Business Review*, *Scientific American* and *MIT Sloan Management Review*. His viral piece on timeboxing is now being featured in HBR Emotional Intelligence Series publication, *Developing Good Habits*, alongside James Clear and other leading experts on forming lasting habits and increasing productivity.

PRAISE FOR *TIMEBOXING*

'Timeboxing really works. For over 30 years I've sought to optimize my work and my life. I thought I had things pretty much figured out. But then I read *Timeboxing*. The impact was immediate and dramatic. My new habit of timeboxing each morning has lifted me to a new level of focus, calm, and productivity. If my Stanford students could read only one book this year, I'd want it to be this one.'

BJ Fogg, author of global bestseller *Tiny Habits: The Small Changes That Change Everything*

'A masterclass in intentional living. This book on timeboxing is essential for anyone seeking focus in a distracted world. I've long championed the benefits of timeboxing, and Marc's book brings it to life.'

Nir Eyal, bestselling author of *Indistractable: How to Control Your Attention and Choose Your Life*

'Timeboxing can help you get things done, but more importantly, it can help you do more of what you love and less of what you hate. As you internalize the lessons of this exceptionally wise book, you'll begin to feel the presence of a coach who's there with you every step of the way.'

Kim Scott, bestselling author of *Radical Candor: How to Get What You Want by Saying What You Mean*

'Now more than ever, effective focus is a problem many, probably most of us, feel. We are confused and overwhelmed on a daily basis. This smart and engaging book presents a deceptively simple, subtly powerful technique for structuring our lives and work to actually get things done. It's a revelation.'

Michael Bhaskar, author of *Curation: The Power of Selection in a World of Excess* and *Human Frontiers*

'*Timeboxing* is an eminently practical book that changed my habits almost immediately – and also changed the way I think about time itself. Box time on your calendar right now to read this book.'

Luke Burgis, author of *Wanting: The Power of Mimetic Desire, and How to Want What You Need*

'Constraint = Freedom. The goal isn't to live a rigid existence but instead a life vibrant with intention and full of what truly matters to you. If you feel like you're floating through life without a plan, read this book.'

Elizabeth Grace Saunders, author of *Divine Time Management*

TIMEBOXING

The Power of Doing One Thing at a Time

MARC ZAO-SANDERS

ST. MARTIN'S
ESSENTIALS
NEW YORK

Published in the United States by St. Martin's Essentials,
an imprint of St. Martin's Publishing Group

TIMEBOXING. Copyright © 2024 by Marc Zao-Sanders. All rights reserved. Printed in the United States of America. For information, address St. Martin's Publishing Group, 120 Broadway, New York, NY 10271.

p. vii, Reprinted by permission of HarperCollins Publishers Ltd. © 1954, J.R.R. Tolkien; p. 40, Extract from John Naughton, 'Steven Pinker: Fight Talk from the Prophet of Peace' (2011) © Guardian News & Media Ltd. 2023; p. 50, Extract from Simon Hattenstone, 'Lady Gaga: Lording it' © Guardian News & Media Ltd. 2023; p. 80, From Peter Drucker, 'What Makes an Effective Executive', *Harvard Business Review*, June 2004; p. 92, 'Cat's in the Cradle', words and music by Sandy Chapin and Harry Chapin, Story Songs, Ltd. (ASCAP) All rights administered by Warner Chappell North America Ltd.; p. 226, Reprinted by permission of HarperCollins Publishers Ltd. © 1954, J.R.R. Tolkien; p. 256, Excerpt from Toni Morrison interview, 'Art of Fiction – No. 134' by *The Paris Review* © 1993, The Paris Review Foundation, Inc, used by permission of The Wylie Agency (UK) Ltd.

www.stmartins.com

The Library of Congress Cataloging-in-Publication Data is available upon request.

ISBN 978-1-250-34015-3 (trade paperback)
ISBN 978-1-250-34016-0 (ebook)

Our books may be purchased in bulk for promotional, educational, or business use. Please contact your local bookseller or the Macmillan Corporate and Premium Sales Department at 1-800-221-7945, extension 5442, or by email at MacmillanSpecialMarkets@macmillan.com.

Originally published in the United Kingdom by Penguin Michael Joseph

First U.S. Edition: 2024

10 9 8 7 6 5 4 3 2 1

To Mama, for literally everything.

Keywords	Intention; agency; serenity; calm; freedom; overwhelm; focus; mindfulness; deep thought; flow; collaboration; planning; trust; to-do list; calendar; ship; rabbit holes; habit; rest; sleep; higher power; one thing; simplicity
Word count	45,142
Read time	226 mins

*All we have to decide is what to do
with the time that is given to us.*

— Gandalf

Contents

Introduction

Our feral ways of working and living do not lead to the chosen, cherished lives we long for. This book is about a practice that does. That practice is called timeboxing.

Why I wrote it

I began my career just over 20 years ago. Back then, I was not in control at all: I took orders as they came, and responded to whoever shouted the loudest. I kept a to-do list but had little idea how to prioritize what was on it. I made basic mistakes, left the most pressing work unfinished and frequently faced disapproval and rebuke. After several months of suffering, I devised a simple system (which I called a daily work plan): select priority items from my to-do list, paste them into a spreadsheet, estimate how long they would take (in units of 7.5 minutes, so they would stack up to quarters, halves and whole hours), and check them off as they were done.

This was much better. The important things were getting done, I could adapt the system as I went, I felt more in control and that I was achieving (the spreadsheet would calculate how many productive hours I had worked each day), and I had a searchable, digital record of my daily endeavours.

But it was still far from perfect. I had to force the spreadsheet to dovetail with existing commitments such as meetings. Colleagues didn't have access to the file (this was the early 2000s, before the advent of Dropbox and Google Drive) and I certainly couldn't invite someone to see the detail behind a particular, single item. Most importantly, the tasks in the spreadsheet didn't relate to the time of day without a lot of manipulation and management: at any given moment it wasn't clear what I should be doing; nor was it clear if I was on track or behind.

A little over 10 years ago, I happened upon an article by Daniel Markovitz in *Harvard Business Review*[1] that suggested that migrating the to-do list to the calendar would have a transformative effect on productivity. Markovitz argued that to-do lists, on their own, are overwhelming, hard to prioritize, lack context and don't commit their owner to them. A shared calendar addressed all of these problems. This resonated. So, in early 2014, I began to adopt the method each and every day and came to know it as timeboxing. First thing every morning, I would spend 15 minutes deciding what to do, and how long I'd do it for and log all this into my Google Calendar.

It changed everything.

I was much more on top of it all. I knew what I was doing and felt confident that these were the right things to be focused on. I was better at predicting when I would complete my tasks and therefore able to say yes or no to new work with justification and confidence. In moments of uncertainty and overwhelm, I had refuge in a mantra I developed, 'Return to calendar', which has been a constant source of light whenever I've needed it. When I started my own business, I wanted to be a transparent and helpful CEO. Timeboxing enabled me to exemplify both with an open, shared record of all I had done and all I was doing for anyone in the team to see.

And I got better at it. When I look back over the past 10 years of calendar entries, I see a reassuring, poignant, instructive evolution of my timeboxing practice: gaps in the working day lessen; the size of the timeboxes becomes more regular; their names become more usefully recognizable; I began to colour code the timeboxes so I could see, at a glance, how much time I was spending in different areas of my life; and as I saw that this systematic approach could be useful outside of work too, more and more of my non-work hours got timeboxed. It really had changed everything.

The method substantially affected what I did and when and how I did it for most of the waking hours of my life. It was indispensable.

Five years on and increasingly enthralled with this new way of life, I wanted others to benefit too. So, I wrote my own article for *Harvard Business Review* (*HBR*) on the subject.[2] Having timeboxed for several years by this point, I had observed some additional benefits that made it even more powerful: seeing projects with colour-coded dependencies at a glance; showing others what I was working on and when; keeping a useful log of all I'd done; being and feeling in control; and simply getting through work faster. That article remained on *HBR*'s Most Popular list for several years. Many readers wrote to me directly. Most just to say that the idea resonated and that they would give it a try. Some said that they had been using the method for a while and were glad to discover it had a name. A single dad told me that it had helped him to cope when life had seemed impossible. Markovitz himself got in touch! And lots asked me directly just how to implement the method.

It didn't just catch on there. In 2022, an enterprising TikTok creator made a video[3] espousing the benefits of the method and featured my article. Within a few weeks, it amassed ten million views. The response to the video provided further evidence of substantial interest in what timeboxing has to offer.

I knew that hundreds of thousands of senior managers already employ personal assistants to timebox for them every day, managing their calendars and increasing their levels of output, comfort and happiness. Many of the world's greatest achievers — Carl Jung, Albert Einstein, Bill Gates and Mary Callahan Erdoes — have employed some version of the practice too.

It seemed that the concept had extraordinarily broad appeal, from Gen Z TikTokers to busy parents to business execs to some of the world's leaders and iconoclasts.

■　■　■　■

Every single weekday morning, a billion or so knowledge workers wake up, gravitate towards a pixelated screen and process information for 8 hours or more. The work is endless. The choice of what to work on is endless. And then there are all our non-work tasks and responsibilities — with their own levels of urgency and importance — which need, somehow, to be juxtaposed and squeezed in.

At any and every given moment, then, we are faced with a sea of non-trivial choices. This causes us to suffer in several ways. We're fatigued by so many always-on options and this diminishes our ability to make the right decisions.[4] We've developed a fear of missing out on all the things we *could* be doing that pop up on social media. Insidious, unseen algorithms determine much of the quality and nature of modern-day experience and just when we break free, untimely, unsolicited notifications draw us back in.

We fail to make space for the habits and activities that will lead us to what we truly long for: self-development, a successful career, fulfilling relationships, good health — a happy, intentional life.

Many of us are therefore more perplexed, bewildered, frazzled, anxious or depressed than we should be. This is the condition of the most privileged people on earth.

In response, thousands of books and articles about productivity and time management have been written. Each has its own angle, often intersecting with some of the others: habits, checklists, focus, flow, energy, prioritization, the promise of doing more with less, anti-procrastination measures, mental health and spirituality. Several of these books offer powerful methods and have become bestsellers: *Deep Work*, *Indistractable*, *Four Thousand Weeks*, *15 Secrets Successful People Know About Time Management*, *Eat That Frog!* and *Atomic Habits*, to name just a few.

And yet none of these books offers a sustained and thorough guide to timeboxing. All six of the aforementioned bestsellers, for example, acknowledge the practice and agree on its potency, but devote just a few paragraphs or pages to it.

So, it seemed that there was an opportunity and responsibility to bring the method and mindset to many more people. This book reveals timeboxing as *the* fundamental time management philosophy, ripe and ready to help the billions of us weighed down by choice every hour of every day.

Ripe and ready to help you.

Why it's for you

Let me guess.

You're busy. You often feel overwhelmed. You live many hours each day digitally, in front of a screen. You own and use several devices that tether you to this digital world. You pick up your phone within minutes of waking up. Your phone charged overnight, next to you, as you slept. You have flexibility in your day, possibly about where you work and probably about what you work on at any given moment. You'd like to develop your skills, to learn, much more than you do. You often find yourself working on several things at once, usually unaware of how that happened, and not feeling good about any of them. You find it hard to keep up with email and messaging apps, often leaving messages unreturned. You don't read as much as you think you should. You carry work worries home and home worries to work. You're often stressed. You don't see the people you love anywhere near as much as you'd like, and you're not fully present when you do. You've tried several productivity techniques and none has worked and stayed. You're dissatisfied with your work-life balance. You're tired. You suspect social media takes more from you than it gives, yet still, you scroll.

You wish you had more time.

Perhaps you are:

- a student struggling with procrastination and meeting deadlines
- a freelancer juggling multiple clients, jobs, finding new work, developing new skills, chasing invoices
- a remote worker managing all that freedom and all those choices
- a creative, needing to reconcile inspiration and artistic expression with hard deadlines and deliverables
- an athlete, cross-fitter or personal trainer, organizing training schedules and diet plans for yourself and your clients

- a parent, balancing work and family and everything else
- a single parent, fighting a thousand battles, seemingly alone
- a writer suffering from writer's block
- an entrepreneur, trying to make ends meet while getting it all off the ground
- a retiree, with a lot of time, suddenly, and not quite sure how you should use it
- an account manager, not feeling like you're giving any of your clients enough consideration
- someone with the traits of or an official diagnosis of ADHD, struggling with focus and attention.

Though each of us has a distinct background, personality and neurobiology, modernity's recipe of globalization, digitalization and interconnectivity has somewhat bounded and homogenized human experience. We live much the same lives and suffer in similar ways.

We could all use a little guidance. We'd all like reliable access to the best version of ourselves. We'd all like to develop better habits. We'd all like to build on our current ways of working and living rather than invoke wholesale change. We'd all like a simple way to make all this happen.

That's why this book is for you.

The timeboxing stories from around the world on page 296 prove that you're not alone and that things can easily get much better. They tell the stories of people from every continent and many walks of life for whom timeboxing has been a source of comfort, productivity and, in many cases, joy. Their stories demonstrate the broad appeal of timeboxing, and I hope some resonate with you.

How to use the book

The book comprises four parts:

- **PART ONE — BELIEVE** is about developing the conviction that timeboxing makes sense for you, that it works and that its benefits are life-changing.
- **PART TWO — PLAN** helps you choose and create the right timeboxes, usually the night or morning before the day you're timeboxing. It's focused on the crucial 15 minutes that determine the following 15 hours.
- **PART THREE — DO** is for when you're in the timeboxes themselves, during the actual working, living, often unpredictable day.
- **PART FOUR — OWN** encourages you to make timeboxing a habit that sticks with you and adapts for you for each third of your life: work, leisure and sleep. This part is intended to ensure that timeboxing works for you over years and decades, not just months.

Timeboxing is a mindset as well as a method. You'll need to recognize the importance of managing time, that you can change your behaviour and that there are many benefits to timeboxing. This is another way of saying that developing a positive attitude and a belief in what you're doing is a crucial part of making time-boxing (and, indeed, any other important behavioural change) stick. PART ONE — BELIEVE will help you effect just such a mind-set. Once you're in the right frame of mind, you'll need a simple and clear explanation of what to do, the steps to take. PLAN and DO will show you just such a method. Finally, in OWN, your mindset will evolve from adoption to iteration and the method will become your own as you learn to tailor timeboxing to your precise and ever-changing requirements.

The book is written and designed to be pragmatic. The chapters are short and accessible: averaging less than 2,000 words, most can be read by almost anyone in under 10 minutes. Such small pockets of time are easily found or carved out from even the busiest of schedules. And there's something exhilarating, isn't there, in the momentum of knocking off chapters? It may appeal to you that the 24 chapters of this book could easily be read in a single month, at the cost of a few minutes a day. Each chapter comes with a pedagogical infusion of metadata to help you get the most out of it. At the beginning: keywords and a quote to prime and prepare you for what's coming. At the end: two sets of bullets, one to recap and review and the other to encourage personal reflection on aspects of the material.

Timebox as you read. You will get more from this book and more from timeboxing if you combine theory with practice. At first, the timeboxes will be imperfect — too big, too small, too many, too few. And you may feel unsure. But you will quickly gain assurance and your timeboxes will improve faster if you do as you learn and learn as you do. *Chapter 14 — This very chapter* is explicitly devoted to this but I encourage you to experiment right away. You'll notice sooner what you find difficult and can look for help for that from the text. You'll be immersed. You don't need any fancy equipment or anyone's help to start timeboxing and there's a quick-start primer in Chapter 1. The word count and estimated reading time at the start of each chapter make the timeboxing of this book easier still. You have no excuse not to! You might even choose — right now — to timebox the reading of the first chapter, which lies less than 2 minutes away. And if you're resisting that suggestion . . . at least notice this and ask yourself why.

As you read and begin to adopt the timeboxing mindset and method and apply it, you'll notice a series of changes. You will feel more in control of your work. You'll develop a greater sense of agency generally. You'll get better at estimating how long work will take. You'll always have an answer to the question 'What should I do now?' You'll spend less time on empty activities that don't matter and compulsive behaviours that do you harm, because you'll be acting out more of your intentions, devised when you were thinking clearly and calmly. You will use the time you previously wasted on one or two activities that matter — a useful language, a long-lost instrument, a long-coveted skill, an overgrown garden, a neglected relationship. Your weekends and vacations will become what you mean them to be. You may find yourself talking about timeboxing to family, friends, even strangers. You'll spend much less time regretting how you've chosen to spend your time. And over time, short-term gains will accrue to life-affirming, life-long change.

You will achieve timeboxing excellence much faster than I did. The 10 years of benefits I've discovered through trial and error can be yours in less than a month. Better still, you'll develop your own version of it, customized for your context and your life.

■ ■ ■ ■

I run a technology business,[5] which, with the rest of life's exigencies, is as consistently exhausting as it is exhilarating. Timeboxing has enabled me to maintain a good degree of control over it all. It helps me choose what to stay on top of, and how to stay on top of just that. Amid the chaos of the day and the call of countless duties, there is a reassuring calm — a *power* — in coming back to one thing at a time.

I believe the method is natural and accessible and can help you to do more, feel better and live the life you choose to lead. I hope that timeboxing will be for you what it has become for me: a life-changing, life-long guide, which brought much-needed peace and productivity to a hurried, haphazard life.

PART ONE — BELIEVE

■ ■ ■ ■

The first part of the book is about understanding
what timeboxing is and developing the conviction
and motivation to change what you decide to do
and when you do it. You will soon understand the
many great benefits of timeboxing and be able to
consider them in the context of your own life.

*One thinks with a watch in one's hand, even as
one eats one's midday meal while reading the
latest news on the stock market; one lives as if
one always 'might miss out on something'.*

— Friedrich Nietzsche

1. Timeboxing is the answer

Keywords	Definition; frazzled; fear of missing out (FOMO); agency; intention; method; mindset
Word count	2,352
Read time	12 mins

What is timeboxing?

Timeboxing is often conflated and confused with similar-sounding approaches to time management: time-blocking, scheduling, daily planning, single-tasking, calendar management and timetabling.

Disparate, inconsistent, overlapping definitions of timeboxing will not do for a book on the topic! They are collectively and individually unsatisfactory. I propose that timeboxing is the method and mindset of:

Selecting what to do, before the day's distractions arise; specifying each task in a calendar, including when it will start and finish; focusing on one thing at a time; doing each to an acceptable (rather than perfect) standard.

This definition accommodates the most important elements of the practice: intentionality, focus, achievement, order, completion and the creation of the timebox itself. It also makes the important point that we should box the time when, and only when, we have the wherewithal to do so. All the rules we make (the law, coding conventions, household policies) as a civilized society are examples of making a set of decisions at the outset, in a moment of cerebral calm and consideration (often by a carefully appointed committee), to help make life smoother in the long run. Timeboxing applies that principle to a special and specific circumstance: you.

Though not quite a definition, an alternative and also useful way of thinking about timeboxing is as a synthesis of your to-do list and your calendar. The to-do list tells us what to do. The calendar tells us when to do it. The combination is much more readily actionable and useful than either on its own.

It's also worth distinguishing timeboxing from time-blocking. Time-blocking is the blocking off of time to do something. Time-boxing is time-blocking + *committing to getting the task done in time*, within the box. In other words, time-blocking is about exclusive focus; timeboxing is exclusive focus + specified outcome.

What problem does it solve?

The problem is that we don't use our time well. We procrastinate. We achieve less than we ought to. We don't feel free, even in our free time. We overcommit. We feel anxious. Most of us exhibit many of the characteristics listed in the Introduction.

We struggle to use our time well today, especially because:

- Knowledge work is never-ending.
- We are constantly faced with many choices. That choice brings an unpleasant pressure to choose well. And most of what we have to choose from is crap; the abundance of choice stems from an abundance of crap.
- We've developed a fear of missing out (FOMO), which

stems from a heightened awareness of what's going on elsewhere, largely served up by social media feeds.

- Control is ceded to algorithms and other people. We have lost a lot of our freedom, our agency.[6]
- We don't have long here — just four thousand weeks, as Oliver Burkeman put it. And we have far fewer for certain special, limited opportunities, such as time with grandparents, grandkids, our dear old parents, our finest friends.

But the question of what we should do at a given moment is a constant. Philosophy has grappled with it through the ages, from Plato's *ethics* to Kant's *hypothetical imperative*[7] to the existentialists wondering about the purpose of being here, and what to do while we are. The question permeates fiction too — consider the plight and behaviour of Camus's Meursault (*L'Étranger*), George Cockcroft's *The Dice Man* or Beckett's Didi and Gogo in *Waiting for Godot*.

There's a simple, compelling logic to the idea that our lives are the cumulative sum of our experiences, and that as a smart species endowed with free will, we can, to a large extent, choose those experiences. Choose well and live a good life. Choose badly, and don't. The problem is that we often choose badly. The problem is that we don't live as good a life as we could.

The features that make timeboxing exceptional

Some of the features of timeboxing demonstrate its inherent strengths, as a mindset and method.

To be clear, features are the characteristics of the method —

what it *is*. Benefits, on the other hand, are the ways in which the method will improve your life. In commercial business parlance: features tell, benefits sell. This chapter is about timeboxing's features, while the remainder of this part of the book focuses on the evidence that it works (see *Chapter 2 — It works*) and the benefits it brings to its devotees (see chapters 3–8).

Timeboxing is **logical**. We systematically decide on the most important aspects of our lives, prioritize them and give them due attention. As we do so, we ensure that our succession of experiences, our use of time, is systematically optimized, hour by hour and day by day. To those of us that do, the question is: how can one *not* timebox?

Timeboxing is **natural**. Specifically, it's a natural *extension* of what we already do. Approximately half of our working lives (meetings, commutes, collaborative work sessions) and some of our leisure time (a driving lesson, a cinema showing, a massage, a restaurant booking) are prearranged with start and end points. Let's say that roughly 4 hours of your working day and 2 hours of your leisure time are already prearranged — 6 hours in total. Timeboxing is simply an extension of this and therefore should feel natural. The practice involves looking at the rest of your waking hours (with the example given, there are approximately 10 left) and encourages you to decide how some of that time would be better spent too. The habit is less of a daunting encumbrance if you think of it as moving from a baseline of 6 up to 8, 10 or 12 time-boxed hours, rather than from a base of zero. Since you timebox already, you can use your existing systems and processes, and over the course of the book we will review and try to improve on these. All this by way of saying, unlike many other self-help methods, timeboxing is not an alien practice — needing to force its way into an already jam-packed life of set ways and established behaviours.

Timeboxing is **actionable**. Add a single item to your calendar, set an appropriate duration, and you're up and running. The approach here is to take the single most effective method, focus entirely on that and fully immerse you in it — learning by doing wherever possible — in order that you master it and make it your own.

Timeboxing is **complementary**. There are many approaches to time management. Timeboxing is not only consistent with them, it's able to support any and all of them. If you have adopted Eisenhower's Matrix (categorizing tasks into a 2 x 2 matrix of important vs urgent), you would take the most important, most urgent items and place them into your timeboxed calendar sooner rather than later. If you believe in eating frogs[8] (getting the most difficult work done at the start of the day), you can place those frogs upfront in your calendar. If you think prioritizing rocks before pebbles and sand (that smaller tasks should be arranged around bigger tasks) then slot them in accordingly, largest first. If you subscribe to the 80/20 rule (that 80% of the consequences derive from 20% of the causes), you will work to identify the vital few and stick them in your calendar ahead of the trivial many. If you are a chunker, chunk away, and timebox the chunks. If you consider your energy levels to be a major driver of your personal productivity, then choose to carry out creative work, administrative tasks, meals, exercises and breaks at the times of day that suit. If nutrition is part of your personal productivity plan, timeboxing will serve up reminders of the snacks or drinks you need, when you need them. Timeboxing is the flexible friend of any and all other time management techniques — the one habit to rule them all. (But notice that many of these techniques do conflict with *each other*: what if your energy levels require you to deal with bigger tasks *later* in the day? What if the ordering of tasks by difficulty does not perfectly align — and, of course, it frequently won't — with an ordering by size or importance?)

Timeboxing is relatively **undiscovered**. The general public searches online for 'timeboxing' much less than they do for other techniques. The terms 'Eisenhower Matrix' and 'Pomodoro Technique', for example, are both searched for many times more than 'timeboxing'. For now, you will be in a relatively small and special minority of timeboxers. The group of adherents who see and enjoy the benefits is growing steadily. And it's not one of those game-theoretical secrets that must be kept by a critical minority in order to preserve its value; timeboxing is a tide that lifts all boats. In fact, the more people who timebox, the greater the collective synchronization and collaborative harmony (see *Chapter 6 — To collaborate*).

Timeboxing basics, so you can start right away

You will get much more from the pages and chapters that follow if you practise timeboxing actively as you read them. I can't squeeze all the benefits, nuances, reasons why and subtle secrets into the first chapter, but here are the very basics, beyond the definition, for you to familiarize yourself and experiment with, from tomorrow, or even today.

You'll need the right mindset. You'll need a positive attitude and a belief that this may work. That you have this book in your hands at all and got this far suggests you are in good shape on this front. Know that the remaining chapters in Part One provide plenty more evidence of timeboxing's wide-ranging benefits.

As for the method, there are two activities that together constitute timeboxing — planning and doing — which correspond to

Parts Two and Three, respectively, of this book. Here's what you need to do for each.

Plan (before the day)

- Set a period of time (15 or 30 minutes), before the busyness of the day clouds your mind and impairs your judgement, to decide what's most important and needs to get done.
- Set a daily (ideally digital) calendar appointment for this planning session, first thing in the morning (or last thing the night before). Make the appointment recur so you won't ever miss it.
- Review your to-do list. If you don't keep one, start! To-do lists feed timeboxing; the better your to-do list, the better your timeboxing.
- Select some of the most important and urgent items from that list and add them to your calendar. Make the best estimate you can about how long each task will take. Don't worry, yet, about the ordering — just get them in.
- Start, make mistakes and learn quickly. To begin with, you will frequently under- or overestimate how long tasks take — this is normal.

Do (during the day)

- Start on time.
- Remove distractions, the most dangerous of which by far is your smartphone.
- Stick to the plan. Don't second-guess yourself and undermine your earlier decision. Barring an emergency,

what you thought earlier in the planning process, when you were calm and clear, is better than what you think to do reactively in the maelstrom of the day.

- Finish on time. Get the job done. Do not permit the perfect to be the enemy of the good. Good is usually good enough.
- Aim to share what you've done as you finish each timebox. This brings a useful pressure to get it done and make it good enough to share — you'll see that this is an important standard to meet.
- You'll get distracted and derailed. Expect this. When it happens, practise coming back to the timebox (return to the calendar), to your original task. With experience, your distractions will become fewer and shorter-lived.

This topic you are reading about, timeboxing, is unusually perfect for experimentation as you go. Every morning you wake and have a brand-new chance to try out what you've learnt, tweak it, experiment with it, question it, make it your own. Do not pass up this opportunity! To ease into it, you might like to try timeboxing *every other* day (Mondays — Wednesdays — Fridays or Tuesdays and Thursdays, say). This sort of arrangement will enable you to contrast a life with timeboxing against a life without. I expect you will soon feel the urge to start timeboxing your non-timeboxed days.

■ ▪ ▪ ▪

So, you should now be clear on what timeboxing is and the features it comes with, out of the box, as it were. And you have had multiple strong encouragements to timebox as you go.

Over the next few chapters, we'll see the evidence that it works, as well as some of the benefits it will bring you. I hope and expect that the combination of timeboxing's inherent strengths and its wide-ranging benefits will persuade you that this is a very special method. It's not just another productivity hack. It's not even just one of the best time management techniques. It's the greatest of all time management methods, the GOAT. It may even be the best possible way for you to live your life.

Review

- The problem timeboxing solves is that we don't use our time well.
- Timeboxing is the practice of:
    - selecting what to do, before the day's distractions arise
    - specifying each task in a calendar, including when it will start and finish
    - focusing on one thing at a time
    - doing each to an acceptable (rather than perfect) standard.
- In a sense, timeboxing is the combination of the to-do list and the calendar.
- You will be able to adopt the mindset and method faster and get much more from this book if you experiment as you read.

Reflect

- What did you think timeboxing was before you decided to read this book?
- Pick one of your other personal productivity methods. How would you make it work with timeboxing?
- How much of yesterday's 16 waking hours would you say you spent well?
- Here's a list of the ten most popular time management techniques and tips. Timeboxing touches on all ten to some extent and is deeply intertwined with eight. Which eight?[9]
    - prioritize tasks
    - create a to-do list
    - use a calendar
    - set deadlines
    - schedule breaks
    - delegate tasks
    - eliminate distractions
    - track your time
    - break down big tasks
    - take advantage of technology.

It is a capital mistake to theorize before you have all the evidence. It biases the judgement.

— Sherlock Holmes

2. It works

Keywords	Trust; credibility; proof; science; evidence; belief; intention; goal; implementation intention; commitment
Word count	2,154
Read time	11 mins

Timeboxing works. I believe it because I have seen it work, for me and many others. As already mentioned, you will need to believe it too, in order to be moved to try it and then embed it into your life. So, let's take one chapter and less than 10 minutes to examine the evidence and see if it convinces you.

Science and implementation intentions

Most time management techniques are based on intuitive hunches that have taken hold, rather than hard science. Timeboxing is based on both. Several scientific papers (largely led by Peter Gollwitzer[10] in the 1990s) indicate that setting out intentions formally ahead of time significantly increases the likelihood of attaining a goal.

Gollwitzer introduced the concept of the *implementation intention*, commitments of the form 'when situation X arises, I will perform response Y'. They are more granular and tangible than the loftier notion of a *goal intention* ('I intend to achieve X') and make up the milestones that lead to the end goal. Implementation intentions are also more practical and useful, specifying what needs to get done, and when and where it will happen.

Timeboxing is a kind of implementation intention. The what, when and where are all specified by you as you timebox properly. And a planned timebox — if made carefully, intentionally and not under duress — will ensure that its completion contributes to the attainment of a worthwhile goal. So, I'm hitching timeboxing onto the implementation intention bandwagon as we consider the scientific evidence for the latter. A timeboxed digital calendar provides just the right digital stimuli (the calendar, synchronized across multiple devices) for us modern knowledge workers to achieve our goals.

How, then, does the evidence for implementation intentions look? Very good. Multiple independent studies (referenced in the Gollwitzer paper) show that the inclusion of an implementation intention radically improves results:

- In one study, a group of university students were asked about projects they would complete over a holiday period. For difficult projects, 67% of participants who had formed an implementation intention had been successful, compared with just 25% who hadn't.
- In another student study, participants were asked to write a report on how they spent their Christmas Eve. Half were told to state on the questionnaire when and where they intended to write the report within the 48-hour period (in other words, to timebox it), the other half were not. 75% of those asked to timebox the task sent a report, whereas just 33% of those without the instruction did so. This indicates the massive effect of merely *asking* someone to timebox. The effect of full timeboxing — selecting and planning the timebox *ourselves* — is bound to be greater still.
- In a totally different field, a study considered women who had set themselves the goal of performing a breast

self-examination (BSE) over the coming month. Among participants who set themselves an implementation intention, 100% carried out the BSE, vs just 53% of those who did not set an intention.

- Similarly impressive results have been found among critical populations — including drug addicts during withdrawal, schizophrenic patients and frontal-lobe damage patients — who have been able to show marked improvements in recovery rates by setting implementation intentions.

- A 2023 study[11] concluded that implementation intentions are effective in reducing self-harm amongst vulnerable people. Implementation intentions therefore represent a useful intervention for reducing self-harm in specified critical situation.

These studies don't just corroborate timeboxing. They quantify the uplift: we are around 2.5 times more productive if we set an implementation intention and a time to achieve it. Few, if any, other time management techniques have been supported by multiple and independent threads of scientific evidence.

You're already doing it

I stated in the previous chapter that most of us are already timeboxing to some extent as we maintain a calendar of scheduled appointments. As we saw in Chapter 1, this means that the practice feels *natural* to us. It also illustrates that timeboxing works. We ourselves schedule meetings with a beginning and end time and others invite us to their meetings. Many of us also box off time for our own tasks: we put on headphones, go for a walk or take a laptop to an alternative environment to get something done.

So, although we may not be timeboxing consciously or very much or optimally, we are all unmistakably headed in that direction. There is no possibility of opting out, because the practice of choosing to act in a particular way at a certain time, often in concert with others, is so fundamental to how human beings go about their lives at work and outside of it. We wouldn't all be doing it if it didn't work. It works. Making it truly intentional, though, is the key to self-mastery and peace of mind.

Furthermore, there's a whole industry that's built up around timeboxing for others. Every day, hundreds of thousands,[12] if not millions, of human assistants carry out tasks for their busy managers. Central to all executive assistant roles are: organizing and maintaining calendars, making appointments and preparing managers for meetings. Otherwise known as timeboxing. Assistance in this way has been a common practice in business for the several decades that knowledge work has eaten the world. Is it even conceivable that hundreds of thousands of people (and now artificially intelligent agents) would be carrying out these valuable duties for their big-time bosses if this were not, in fact, a valuable activity?

Expert consensus

As we saw in the Introduction, many productivity gurus point to timeboxing, while several of the foremost productivity experts all quietly advocate for the method (though they use different names for it).

In the last few years, Big Tech has spotted and jumped on this trend. Google, through its Time Insights feature, demonstrates to users exactly how they're spending their time. Similarly, Microsoft's Viva Insights offers users multiple perspectives on how they are allocating their time during the workday, in the interests of increasing productivity and improving wellness. These tech giants are not alone; several smaller platforms and start-ups have woken up to and are capitalizing on the opportunity (more in *Chapter 23 — Tools & tech*).

In a meta-study[13] of productivity tips carried out by my company, Filtered, timeboxing topped the list of the productivity techniques recommended by experts:

1	Timeboxing	22	Write it down
2	Prioritize	23	Break tasks down
3	Say no	24	80/20 Rule
4	Move!	25	Be true to yourself
5	Control your devices	26	Avoid visual distractions
6	Take short breaks	27	Sleep
7	To-do lists	28	Run meetings well
8	Eat well	29	Batch similar tasks
9	2-minute rule	30	Fewer meetings
10	Control social media	31	Focus on outcomes
11	Choose when to check email	32	Effective above efficient
12	Organize your workspace	33	Delegate
13	Start earlier	34	Ignore the news
14	Breathe	35	Change the scenery
15	Turn off alerts	36	Long breaks
16	Shorter meetings	37	Time yourself
17	Site blockers	38	Be positive
18	Productivity tools	39	Follow up after meetings
19	Plan ahead	40	One small change
20	Single-tasking	41	Flow
21	Sounds & music	42	Drink water

43	Drink coffee responsibly	72	Visualize success
44	Make a public commitment	73	Reward yourself
45	Acknowledge your success	74	Rituals
46	Don't reread emails	75	Eric Schmidt's '9 Rules of Email'
47	Help others in meetings	76	Be flexible
48	Be on time	77	Log all your ideas
49	Kill your darlings	78	Take control when you can
50	Work from home	79	Make work fun again
51	Productive procrastination	80	Natural light
52	Your biological prime time	81	Learn to touch type properly
53	Find time for yourself	82	Listen actively
54	Be realistic	83	Inbox Zero
55	Set clear goals	84	Voicemail
56	Just start	85	Templates
57	Devices in meetings	86	Hard stuff first
58	Break bad habits	87	Close open loops in your head
59	Love your job	88	Waiting-on list
60	Show compassion	89	Deprioritize the non-essential
61	Focus on the present	90	Reply by . . .
62	Systemize	91	Control your inbox
63	Start and end on time	92	Wear a uniform
64	Get ergonomic	93	Set deadlines
65	Use your commute	94	Assign a 'Task Deputy'
66	Unplug	95	Password manager
67	Meeting roles	96	Schedule 'stress' time
68	Do not do to-do lists	97	Five goals
69	10,000 hours	98	Convert emails to to-dos
70	Find lost hours	99	Old-school alarm clocks
71	Short- and long-term goals	100	Chewing gum

Notice that many of the items on the list touch on and are touched on by timeboxing. How many can you spot?

A personal testimony

I will vouch for it. I've been timeboxing for 10 years, having evolved from no good method at all, through to-do lists, a daily work plan and, finally, most happily, to timeboxing.

That's 10 years of *intensive* practice. On average, I create 15 timeboxes per weekday and 5 on the weekend. That adds up: I've made 44,000 timeboxes, i.e. made 44,000 decisions that a particular task/job/activity was the right one for a particular period, and, for the vast majority, I've completed them. That's plenty of practice and experience to determine whether it works for me. And it does. To put it another way, I used to feel much less sure about the day ahead; it was something that would happen *to* me. Now, thanks to timeboxing, it's more like I make the day ahead — and each and every day — happen. The positive feeling also works in retrospect: after periods in which I've timeboxed, I feel happy, both in the accomplishment of the task as well as the satisfaction of a plan coming together.

While I timebox I'm often simultaneously implementing some other productivity methods, too. I maintain an active to-do list (and I object to the calls to 'kill the to-do list' that continue to do the rounds — more on this in Chapter 10). I observe my own energy levels and recognize that, especially for creative or intellectually challenging tasks, I'm much more productive early in the day. Ever since I heard about them, I've been influenced by both the 80/20 Rule (also called Pareto's Principle, that most effects derive from a small set of causes — 20% of authors make 80% of book sales, say) and Parkinson's Law (work expands to fill the time allotted for its completion — if you give yourself 2 hours to write a short paragraph, you'll use all that time). The fact that all these methods dovetail so nicely with timeboxing strengthens my resolve to continue.

Some people consider me to be highly organized, even disconcertingly so (on catching a glimpse of one of my back-to-back, box-to-box timeboxed days, a pained expression followed by an incredulous question: 'How can your life be like that?'). This may be true, but disconcertingly organized people weren't born that way. They've developed and honed a system of self-management that works for them. Very often — and more often than you may think, or they might know — that system is timeboxing.

Over the past decade, I've discussed timeboxing with many colleagues, clients, friends, even strangers. Though clearly invested in the practice, I like to think that I remain open to hearing a convincing objection. I have not. The most convincing objection, to my mind, is that there are some situations to which timeboxing is not well suited. And this I concede and embrace (in *Chapter 24 — It's working*). Timeboxing has, for me personally, stood the test of time.

Most recently, I wrote this book. When the publisher approached me, I was already stretched, with a full-on family and bustling business. The only way to fit another major project into my life was to timebox, even more deliberately and deftly than before. Indeed, some of the finer points written out in these pages were honed in the writing of them — another one of those tales that grew in the telling.

■ ■ ■ ■

I hope you are becoming convinced. Full conviction will only be achieved as you start to fill your own calendar with your events/implementation intentions/timeboxes. These opening two chapters have described the problem we face, the solution timeboxing provides and the evidence that it works. Over the next six, we'll cover the most important benefits of the method, presented in a past—present—future framing.

Review

- The evidence that timeboxing works comes from multiple sources.
- Timeboxing is a form of implementation intention (when situation X arises, I will perform response Y), a method for which there is plenty of scientific evidence.
- We all already timebox, to some extent.
- Many leading productivity experts with disparate agendas agree that timeboxing works.

Reflect

- Recall a situation in which you were presented with evidence that changed your mind on an important issue. What was it that convinced you?
- Make an implementation intention now.
- There are types of evidence presented in this chapter that timeboxing works. Which is the most persuasive to you? Why?

Cognitive psychology tells us that the unaided human mind is vulnerable to many fallacies and illusions because of its reliance on its memory for vivid anecdotes rather than systematic statistics.

— Steven Pinker

3. For the record

Keywords	History; log; record; memory; search; reflection; learning; self-knowledge; self-awareness
Word count	1,304
Read time	7 mins

The first benefit to timeboxing is about the past — your past.

Since the advent of the internet, we've kept a record of our day-to-day lives in the form of our search history and social media posts. Unfortunately, the chief beneficiary of this record has been Big Tech (Alphabet [Google], Amazon, Apple, Meta [Facebook] and Microsoft) rather than you. Timeboxing, at last, allows you to create a record of great personal use to you alone.

A timeboxed calendar is a log of what you've done for much, maybe even most, of your day. To repurpose Lincoln's Gettysburg Address, it's of you, by you and for you. This information can be invaluable to you in several ways.

Memory

What were you up to last Tuesday afternoon? When did you last speak to that old school friend you don't see nearly enough of? How long have you been running your weekly team meetings? How long has it been since you met with that promising sales prospect?

It's alarming how quickly we forget what we do. Many of us struggle to remember what we did earlier today, much less yesterday, or last week. This may be a function of cramming so much into our lives that there's too much to recall and too little mental capacity left to recall it.

Well, timeboxing provides an answer to this. It's a searchable log of as much of what you've done as you choose to record. For me, I'm able to retrieve information about the vast majority of my waking life over the past decade. Sometimes this will be a particular piece of information (a name, a phone number, a did-I-do-that-or-didn't-I?) and sometimes the relevant timebox will jog a whole host of richer memories about a past event or activity. Either way, a timeboxed log for ready reference has tangible uses.

Such information can be invaluable when you're in a defensive mode. Suppose there's a difficult situation at work and you need to be able to show what you did and when. A timeboxed calendar with all the relevant entries enables you to respond without doubt and without delay.

A record can also help us manage health. Knowing when you fell, when you first started taking the medication or when you last saw that specialist can be a lifesaver, or at least a well-being enhancer, in certain circumstances. It's worth marking these incidents, accidents and appointments in your calendar.

But it's far more common and likely that a timeboxed log will reap *positive* rewards. Here's one example. You have a meeting coming up with someone you've not seen for quite a while. You suspect you have some useful handwritten notes from your last meeting with them but you can't find the notes because you can't remember when that meeting took place. Well, a timeboxed calendar enables you to find — via a simple name or email search — when that meeting was, in order to pinpoint and surface the entry in your notes.

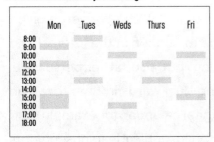

An untimeboxed week: just meetings

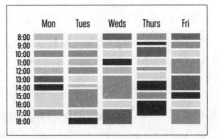

A timeboxed week: a treasure trove of memories

You can easily further enhance your search capability. If you're consistent with the terms you use (maybe even follow the hashtag convention) in titles and descriptions of your timeboxes, a simple search in your calendar will tell you when and how often you were engaged on #sales, #family, #meditation, #1-1s, etc. More on this in *Chapter 11 — Box-making*.

Motivation

Timeboxing provides a record of what you've done — your achievements. That can motivate you to get even more done. Some like to add an emoji tick (✅) to calendar entries as they complete them. The dopamine rush that this can give feels rewarding and motivates us to do it again. It's such a positive experience that creating timeboxes after the fact (between 9:00am and 9:30am I did this, from 10:00am to 11:00am I did that, etc.) is often worthwhile (and contributes, of course, to the searchable log). Several productivity experts extol the virtues of maintaining a 'done list'. Well, timeboxing ticks that box too. By keeping a record and thereby measuring our achievements, we get an immediate reward in the moment, a dopamine hit that motivates us to do it again (this is, of course, in addition to the larger, longer-term benefits that carrying out the task brings).

A mantra of some hard-line timeboxers is, 'If it's not in the calendar, it doesn't exist', i.e., that unless it's timeboxed, a given activity is very unlikely to be made to happen in the future. I find this particular phrasing off-putting, but also rather persuasive. And the logic is compelling going backwards in time too: if an event hasn't been logged (in a digital calendar, for example), did it really happen? Whichever your philosophical leanings,[14] events that are neither recorded nor remembered did not exist or happen in a way that's of any use to anyone.

Another motivating perspective is that a well-logged life may *feel* better. Among others, Sean Carroll, the physicist and philosopher, has argued[15] that the more memories we accumulate, the more time seems to have elapsed. A life loaded full of memories, not just activities, may feel to us like a fuller, richer, more worthwhile adventure.

Self-development

A timeboxed calendar can help us to reflect on how we've been living our lives. It can help us to answer potentially important reflective questions such as:

- What else was on my mind the day I made that big decision?
- Have I been working too hard?
- Have I spent enough time on aspect XYZ of my life?
- What good or bad habits are recurring and need to be addressed?
- How and how often do I indulge myself?

- What have been my proudest moments recently?
- Do I pay enough attention to my partner?

You may never love your timebox more than on that day each year when it's time to fill in your performance review with all that you've achieved over the past 12 months. The simple act of including the hashtag #review (say) in relevant boxes as you go will make your life incalculably easier and prevent you from forgetting important accomplishments.

Of course, much of the material recorded as timeboxes in your calendar will be mundane (so, think about how to liven it up: notes to your future self, jokes, captivating titles, etc.) But there is also value in the mundane; as the novelist Ian McEwan says, 'The banalities begin to shine after many years have passed.'[16]

Economy

You may already keep other written records. Journaling,[17] bullet journaling, notes and even email all log activity in their way. But timeboxing is especially economical. It takes a matter of seconds to create a basic, operative timebox. And it's not just quick, it's also easy, because almost all of us already use a digital calendar.

■　■　■　■

A personal record of what you did and when is useful and grounding, and can provide insights about yourself and others. It's private and intimate, so keep it to yourself and for yourself.

Review

- Timeboxing creates a searchable log of what you've done.
- It can be used to
    - retrieve information and jog your memory
    - gain credit and motivate you to persevere
    - allow you to reflect and grow.

Reflect

- Pick one of the seven self-development questions from this chapter that strikes you as particularly relevant. See if you can find a new truth about yourself.
- Have you had a situation at work in which you wished you had a better means of recalling what happened on a particular day?
- What were you doing this time yesterday? Close your eyes and just try to remember, unaided. Notice what your mind throws up as you try to pull out this specific information.
- What were you doing this time last week? Again, close your eyes and just try to remember, unaided. And again, notice what your mind throws up as you try to pull out this specific information.

*I am my own sanctuary and I can be reborn
as many times as I choose throughout my life.*

— Lady Gaga

4. For serenity

Keywords	Stress; worry; overwhelm; suffering; agency; control; satisfaction; happiness; enlightenment; liberation; peace; sanctuary
Word count	1,384
Read time	7 mins

Timeboxing can make you feel less stressed and more in control. It can liberate you. The chief benefit of timeboxing, for me, lies in this chapter: the most substantial gain to be had, I've found, is in mental wellness, ahead even of productivity. This chapter is about the emotional and psychological advantages of timeboxing.

We're agreed that modern knowledge workers are anxious and overwhelmed. The statistics bear this out too: 15% of working adults are estimated to have a mental disorder; globally, 12 billion working days are lost every year to depression and anxiety, which costs US$1 trillion in lost productivity.[18]

By guiding all of us back to a single activity at any given time, amid the chaos of the day and the thousand other things we might do, timeboxing keeps us focused and centred. As distractions mount — and this is especially true of incoming communications — your timeboxed calendar can become a refuge to find solace, reassured that what you have prioritized is what you should be doing, and all you should be doing for that time.

Focus when not timeboxing   Focus when timeboxing

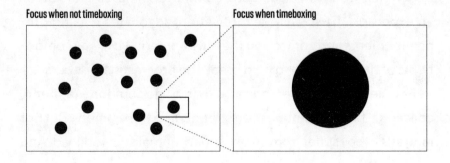

Suffer less

Are you a perfectionist? A procrastinator? A people-pleaser? A multitasker? Or a worrier? Perhaps you show flashes of several of these personas at different times. Almost everyone does. I do. Modernity, with all its technological vastness and permanent interconnectivity, provokes these sorts of characteristics and tendencies. Unfortunately, all these tendencies lead to suffering. Fortunately, timeboxing guides us elsewhere.

In striving to achieve the impossible, perfectionists are constantly correcting and iterating, never quite content to draw a line under the task at hand. Deadlines are therefore missed and extensions requested. By evaluating their own work harshly and perceiving similar assessments from others, they rarely feel satisfied. Timeboxing can rescue the perfectionist by drawing that line with the contour of the timebox, and insisting that at a certain point in time, something *must* be delivered, sent on, shared, shipped (see *Chapter 17 — Ship something*).

Procrastinators leave tasks until the last minute, despite knowing that doing so will likely entail negative consequences. This usually leads to lower-quality output. It's also correlated with depression, anxiety and low self-esteem.[19] Timeboxing can help at least the mild procrastinators to jump-start their productivity and begin their work earlier, at a pre-committed time. Dr Piers Steel, an expert on the science of motivation, advocates making pre-commitments and controlling the environment — two key components of timeboxing — to help break the procrastinator's curse.

People-pleasers over-promise to indulge someone (a friend, colleague, family member, even strangers) in the moment. But not long after, they suffer from an expanded, unrealistic workload. And soon after that they encounter the dissatisfaction and disappoint-ment of colleagues. Timeboxing can help people-pleasers to say no with proper justification and at the right time, by providing hard data on what time they actually have available. Indeed, it may even pre-empt the request if the calendar is already shared (and busy).

Multitaskers try to get more done by doing more than one thing at once. But they rarely can. Not only is multitasking negatively correlated with performance,[20] but studies have also shown that it makes people feel less positive. This happens all the time: we're looking for our keys but a book we once meant to read hijacks our attention; we're emailing someone and a separate, vexing email catches our eye; we're reading one of the Narnia Chronicles to a child and a smartphone notification wrenches us out of that world. Anti-multitasking measures (such as batch emailing — a dedicated period of exclusively working on your inbox) have been shown to improve well-being.[21] Timeboxing, as a single-tasking method, is a good way of avoiding this bad habit. For the nuance to multi-tasking, see Chapter 18.

Worriers worry and suffer, therefore, by definition. Even when worriers are productive — and they often are — there are many complex, negative downstream ramifications for mental health, both professionally and socially. Timeboxing is not a silver bullet here, but some people with this affliction have found comfort in scheduling specific, dedicated worry time.[22] Set aside a period to ponder over an issue and you might find this compartmentaliza-tion frees you up to get on with the rest of life, before and after that time. Timeboxing is also a perfectly pragmatic means of taking a small, single step in a positive direction when we're feeling low.

Increase your very own agency

Agency is the feeling of control over your actions and their consequences. Plenty of ancient and modern wisdom centres around focusing on the things we can control, rather than trying to exert a wider influence and feeling disappointed when we fail. Timeboxing is a pragmatic means of applying this guidance.

As a feeling, agency is difficult to quantify and calibrate. But not impossible. A study of 36,000 people from 33 European countries concluded that 'both choice and opportunity enhancing societal conditions and an individual's perceived autonomy are positively associated with life satisfaction.'[23] It makes sense. Our species, having evolved on the basis that only the fittest survive, is programmed to want to control its environment, to survive and thrive. And it makes intuitive sense too: when I feel in control, I feel happier; when I'm not in control, I am less so. As Jeff Bezos has put it: 'Stress primarily comes from not taking action over something you can have some control over.'[24] Increased agency adds to our sense of well-being, and we owe it to ourselves to seek it out.

Timeboxing gets you out of other people's agendas and into and onto your own. Your inbox is a list of requests and information that other people decided to put on your plate. The meetings you're invited to are to discuss other people's ideas, aspirations and plans. The dozens of notifications you get every day are intrusions from external agents (whether from people or automated). None of this is *your* agenda. Some of it may coincide with your agenda. But it's not been crafted that way, by design. Only you can carve out your own path, and timeboxing is the most effective means of achieving this. Do you want your legacy to be that you lived your life at the beck and call of others? Well, if you choose to do what matters to you at the times of your own choosing, it becomes your beck and call, your increased agency.

Timeboxing also provides the right *kind* of agency. You choose what you do. And you make those choices when you are in the right state to do so. It must be a greater and better feeling of control if it's over the kinds of actions that you have properly considered, in the calm before the storm of the day, when you were at your unruffled, unfettered best.

Set yourself free

Timeboxing can be liberating. Reducing stress and increasing agency are both important but even collectively they understate the benefits of the method. Timeboxing can be transformative. By saying yes to one thing, you are unburdening yourself enormously, by saying no to a thousand others. Seeing and appreciating this is supremely enlightening and liberating.

Timeboxing can even be thought of and practised as a life guide. It's a reassuring voice (your own) that you can trust (the thinking was done when you were clear-headed), which reminds you of what you should be doing at any given moment of your day. Of course, you will occasionally get detached and distracted from that voice. But you know where it is (a single click away) and can come back to it 24/7, whenever you need it. That voice is a secular higher power, which can be with you throughout your life if you choose to seek it out and listen to it.

Review

- Timeboxing helps with mental health just as much as it helps with personal productivity.
- Through timeboxing you get to choose exactly what you want to do, as opposed to being at the beck and call of others.
- The experience of saying yes to one thing at a time and no to everything else at that time can be immensely liberating.

Reflect

- Is it more important to you to *feel* better or *perform* better?
- When do you feel the most stress? Jot down some of the characteristics of those situations. Is it often when several things are happening to you at once?

That brain of mine is something more than merely mortal; as time will show.

— Ada Lovelace

5. To think smarter

Keywords	Flow; capability; clarity; priming; planning; epiphany; insight; mental capacity; deep work; remembering
Word count	1,675
Read time	8 mins

For good or ill, human beings have been able to dominate Planet Earth because of their brain power. Our species is labelled (admittedly, by us) as Homo *sapiens* (meaning wise or astute). In modern times, a billion of us earn a living as knowledge workers and decision makers. Over the past few years, Smart Thinking (books aimed at helping readers to improve their thinking processes and make smarter, more informed decisions in their personal and professional lives) has become a bona fide book genre. We should take thinking seriously and make the most of our greatest gift — arguably evolution's crowning achievement.

This chapter is about how timeboxing can help us think, live and work smarter, rather than harder. It's about how to achieve quality of output rather than quantity in input. In *Chapter 7 — For productivity* we'll investigate how the method also helps us to achieve *more*.

Thinking is one of those human activities that though immediately accessible to all, is hard to pin down. Whole books and lifetimes are devoted to the subject, so I will just draw one distinction here and then propose to dissolve it. On the one hand, there is *cognitively demanding activity* and on the other there is *thinking*. Cognitively demanding work — coding, writing, designing, editing, reviewing — is somewhat specific and tends to have an explicit, intended outcome. But *thinking* is more diffuse and general and has many varieties including, but not limited to, critical thinking, design thinking, problem-solving, analytical thinking, strategic thinking and decision-making. But for the purposes of this chapter and this book, I will assume that both types of mental activity are important and desirable and argue that timeboxing helps with each.

Seeding

The harvest won't just happen. We can't expect that all the creative spark, imagination and inspiration we'll need for a task is going to come to us in the narrow, specifically time-bounded period we have for it — our timebox. For creative and difficult tasks especially, we need to improve our odds by setting the subconscious and conscious mind to work well before we roll our sleeves up, sit down and get to work. We can, and should, prime our minds by pulling together the relevant information, facts, scattered thoughts, recollections and notes on the topic, take a look at them and then relax and let the subconscious mind do with it what it will.

Suppose you need to write a business plan on Thursday morning, set a timebox to review the information you have (a current draft, your notes, the instruction from your boss, some desk-based research, your company's business plan template, that stellar business plan a colleague wrote and was praised for last month, a generative AI's attempt at writing it) for half an hour on Tuesday afternoon. Then give your mind those 36 hours and a couple of sleeps in between to make better sense of it all. On Thursday morning, you will write a much better plan, faster.

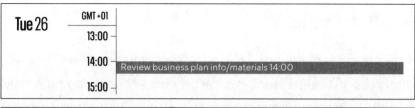

Timeboxing can make us smarter in meetings too. Meetings constitute around one-fifth[25] of our time. Whether we like them or not, they're here to stay, so let's get better at them. If you seed your mind and prepare for all meetings as a rule — for example, by setting a standing Meetings Prep timebox each morning (of 15 or 30 minutes for the handful of meetings you have that day; of course, some important meetings will require additional, dedicated preparation time) — you will always be prepared, appear prepared and excel in them. You will be a more valuable colleague and that will reap rewards in terms of your ideas, contribution and reputation.

Seeding my own mind with ideas has been one of the practical principles on which I've got difficult things done for a decade, including, to be sure, the writing of this book. I never sit down to write cold; I simply don't trust that I will be able to muster the right ideas and words. Instead, I timebox multiple short sessions well in advance, in which I gather my thoughts and research, take a look at it all together without any particular exertion or pressure, give my subconscious a day and a night to process, and only after that set out to write.

The art of planning

Timeboxing is made up of two activities: planning (Part Two) and doing (Part Three). Planning is the process of deciding which tasks to do, how big they are and when to do them. Doing is the process of carrying out that intention, within the specified timebox.

Planning is both a cognitively demanding task and an act of thinking. It's important decision-making. If we do it badly, we'll end up spending time on lower-value pursuits; we'll waste our time. The 15 minutes we might spend setting up our timeboxes each morning substantially affect the following 15 hours we spend in execution. That's 15 minutes of planning time to ensure that 15 hours of life is lived productively — a factoring of 60x. So, it's a crucial activity, which requires cool, calm quiet to get done right. Like revenge, productivity is a dish best served cold.

We can think about the benefits of planning in terms of the benefits of rules. As we saw in Chapter 1, when we set rules we make some important decisions at the outset, which, being made in a period of calm and by the right people, are more likely to be good decisions and good rules. And since we have already decided on these rules, we don't need to second-guess ourselves all the way through the day. Planning a timebox is like this. Once you've decided on your timeboxes in the right conditions, you should be confident that the tasks you've set for that day are indeed the right ones. You've thereby also done away with that nagging doubt about whether you should be working instead on countless other errands at any given moment — you've already decided it. No further deliberation is necessary or welcome. And if the nagging doubt persists, you know to just go back to your timeboxed calendar for the final say. Life is so much simpler.

While reading this chapter, it's quite possible that mindfulness and meditation occurred to you. If so, you will enjoy Chapter 20.

Being brilliant

Timeboxing can help you to scale the heights of your capability. It can be used to engineer the conditions you and your brain need to be at their very best. That means seeding and planning, as above, and also setting up your physical environment right (see *Chapter 9 — The basics*).

If we get all that right, we will indeed cut out distractions and achieve greater focus. By allowing us to focus on one activity at a time, timeboxing will also cut out *stress*, which has been shown to reduce performance. Neuroscientist Daniel Levitin reminds us that multitasking is stressful, as indicated by increased secretion of cortisol and adrenaline, and cites[26] work showing that distractions cost us approximately 10 IQ points.

But better yet, on occasion, timeboxing helps to yield very special levels of quality. Achieving a state of flow (the concept introduced by Csíkszentmihályi, the Hungarian psychologist) or deep work (Cal Newport's idea) requires virtually identical conditions, which are all provided through timeboxing:

- unrelenting focus
- a clear goal
- an immersive experience during which time can feel distorted
- the challenge—skill balance — the task shouldn't be either too easy or too hard.

Timeboxing can raise us to higher levels of creativity and brilliance that we would find difficult to attain without it.

Retrieving information, gathering insight

We are spoilt with powerful technology. The internet provides us with near-infinite information. Smartphones put everything within reach, at all times. The two technologies, together, connect us with billions of other people (the majority of the world now has a smartphone). More recently, Large Language Models (LLMs) provide the capability to generate meaningful, useful text so that we can focus on more human tasks. All of these tools serve to amplify and augment human intelligence and capability.

But there's a specific, especially germane source of information that these vast systems miss, for the most part: our personal histories. As we saw in *Chapter 3 — For the record*, the searchable log that timeboxing provides is not just a log but also a means of prompting our own memories. Utilizing this facility can make us not only *look* smarter than those who are less systematic but also actually *think* smarter (recall better, make broader connections, reach our potential). To get a sense of just how evocative this can be, take a look at your not-so-recent Google search history; I fancy that it will be surprising, empowering, intriguing, inspiring or poignant.

■ ■ ■ ■

To timebox well is to think smarter. And thinking is a lot of what it is to be human. What more could you ask for? Well, perhaps to think smarter along with other minds.

Review

- Timeboxing can help with both cognitively demanding work and general thinking.
- Use the method to seed ideas ahead of when the work needs to be done, thereby activating the subconscious mind.
- Planning the timeboxes is an important decision-making activity with major implications for the productivity of the rest of the day.
- When you are in the timebox, doing it, you have an opportunity to achieve exceptional levels of clarity and depth.
- If you timebox meticulously, you will have a searchable log of information to support you anytime you need to recall a fact or jog a memory. Think smarter by remembering better.

Reflect

- When was the last time you were in a state of flow? What gets you into a state of flow?
- What was the last light-bulb or eureka moment you had? Do you remember what circumstances or conditions helped facilitate it?
- Take a look at your online search history (for most people, this will be from Google) from a few months or years ago. What do you find out? How does it make you feel? Is any of it at all useful to you now?

All for one, one for all.

— Alexandre Dumas

6. To collaborate

Keywords	Harmony; efficiency; social; transparency; trust; coordination; relationships; teamwork
Word count	1,337
Read time	7 mins

Timeboxing is not just about personal productivity. For most of us, collaboration in teams (in and outside your organization, with your clients and suppliers, among your family and friends) is an essential part of modern work and life. Timeboxing suits these dynamics too.

I'm an advocate of the concept of *productive harmony*. The idea is that interacting with others in the right way — straightforwardly, proactively, sensitively and positively — is beneficial for both the engine and the heart of business and home life. It's far more efficient for communication to be straightforward and proactive. And people are likely to be more receptive when the interaction is sensitive and positive. In this way, we do much to avoid the dispiriting, anxiety-inducing and productivity-destroying conflict that afflicts too many human relationships. Timeboxing can help with this soft but salient side of things.

Time, and its quality of synchronicity, enable us to thrive as social creatures. We share enjoyment of events together, like sports matches, shows, concerts, weddings, yes even business meetings, and millions of other human-created occasions, with start and (usually) end times. Timeboxing promotes shared occasions, big and small, thereby helping us to thrive.

The shared, digital calendar

Shared calendars have become a staple of modern life. Apple, Google and Microsoft, in particular, have understood that they need to make their calendar software talk to each other. It's now straightforward to share a calendar with the people you choose irrespective of your or their choice of technologies. They are visual, intuitive and accessible.

Most of us — a 2018 survey[27] put it at 70% of adults — use a digital calendar. That number has likely increased since then.

Note that all the benefits described in this chapter will only be enjoyed by those that use a *shared, digital* calendar. A paper-based system (calendar, notepad, even dedicated timeboxing planners) sits on your desk and your desk alone. If you work in a silo, that may be just fine. If you want to or need to collaborate, take the small step to digitize this aspect of your life. Sharing is caring.

Like clockwork

When shared calendars are used well, much of the potency of timeboxing is uncorked.

The placement of tasks relative to each other becomes much easier. For example, if your child has after-school activities and these are placed in a shared family calendar, everyone with access will be able to coordinate drop-offs, pick-ups and other logistics more easily. The information in the calendar helps everyone to be able to contribute in a way that works and to mark that contribution in the calendar. The result is beneficial for the family's shared interests, as well as for harmonic familial relationships. Of course, there are specific programs (task management software) that deal with this explicitly and automatically. But most of us don't use task management software at all and none of us use the same software in all the different groups (different departments, friends, family) with which we need to collaborate.

Timeboxing provides reassurance that the work will get done. Suppose you ask someone to do something for you, to take a look at a reference you've written, say. If the response is the curt but common 'will do', you might feel slightly reassured. But if the response is 'Sure — timeboxed for Friday 10 am' and you can even see it appear in their calendar, you'll feel entirely reassured and start to appreciate this colleague and their robust and considerate ways of working. How much easier interpersonal relationships and pledges might be if 'timeboxing' became part of the lexicon.

People you trust can even place items as timeboxes in your calendar if they've been permitted to do so. This happens with meetings, and general tasks are an obvious, easy and natural extension of that. To make this all run smoothly, you need to include the right level of information and instruction in the calendar appointment. We'll come to that in Chapter 11.

I have one more benefit to share and I concede that some readers will not like it. The Hawthorne effect is the phenomenon that people may work better and more efficiently if they know that they are being observed. Well, a shared calendar is a modern way of being, potentially, digitally observed by multiple people at any time. People can see what you've done, what you're doing, what you're planning and when. This makes your calendar a kind of commitment device. It can be a curse but, for many, the very existence of such a public commitment can help overcome procrastination and bring the benefits that come with a clear conscience!

Building trust

Shared calendars won't be possible in all situations. You need to have a culture of trust, and an understanding of privacy and privacy settings. And if this is at your company, it will help to have a cooperative IT department.

'Transparency' is a glibly touted buzz word, and full transparency may not even be exactly what you're after. Before you share your calendar, be sure of what you want to share and with whom. Most digital calendars provide a range of privacy settings from zero through partial (appointments may simply indicate that you're busy) to full disclosure. You may also be able to choose which individuals or teams get which setting. Be aware that users with higher privileges (managers, admins, super-admins) may be able to see more than you intend. To get totally comfortable, you might like to check permissions face to face; ask someone you trust what they see when they look at your calendar and confirm it's what you expected.

There's a balance to be struck between privacy settings and calendar management. If you want to include lots of personal details and notes in your appointments, you may need to be tighter with your settings. On the other hand, if you're less effusive you can be more relaxed with them. I hope you don't feel the need to configure all that much.

Deepening relationships

At their best, shared calendars can build and deepen relationships too. This won't be for everyone or all contexts, but if you're comfortable sharing the occasional personal and not-quite-essential work information as timeboxes (a book, a swim, a school run, an art class, a cinema outing), you may get to know colleagues better, in an easy, informal, low-key, unasked-for way. It could be used as an icebreaker for a first interaction or it might fuel the next conversation. We share so much on social media — usually unquestioningly, sometimes recklessly — why not consider sharing a little written detail with a much smaller, presumably more trustworthy group, via a shared calendar?

■　■　■　■

With a digital calendar and a little trust, the collaborative benefits of timeboxing are huge. Digital calendars are easy to effect, trust less so. But most people have enough trust in the people around them to make timeboxing work.

Review

- Timeboxing enhances collaboration as well as personal productivity.
- A shared digital calendar is the best tool to get the most out of timeboxing.
- Timeboxing makes it easier to strategically place tasks relative to each other and provides reassurance between colleagues that work will get done.

- Think about what the right balance between privacy and convenience is with respect to your shared-calendar settings. Do you feel that you can put personal activities in there?
- Including personal timeboxes in your calendar can help break the ice and build relationships.

Reflect

- How many people at work do you trust completely to know what you're doing and when? Think about who they are.
- Have a think about who you don't trust and why.
- Outside of work, who might benefit from knowing your schedule better? Think close family, extended family, friends, volunteering organizations, neighbours.
- If you use the phrase 'will do', consider changing it, at least sometimes, to 'timeboxed for [time]'.
- There are many common, imprecise words and phrases about timing: soon, shortly, ASAP, in a while, before long. Which of these do you use? Would more precise language be better in some situations?

Effective executives differ widely in their personalities, strengths, weaknesses, values, and beliefs. All they have in common is that they get the right things done.

— Peter Drucker

7. For productivity

Keywords	Productivity; prioritize; vital few; 80/20; quantify; multitasking; distraction; interruption; social media
Word count	1,756
Read time	9 mins

It has become unfashionable to talk about productivity. These days, the idea is tinged with negative associations, such as micro-management, the doomed pursuit of never-ending tasks, and a disregard for work—life balance and mental wellness. But I have no qualms when it comes to stating and arguing that the aspiration to achieve more is still relevant, important and honourable, at work and at home alike. And timeboxing helps us do that.

Making the right choices

As Drucker says,[28] we get more done mostly by focusing on the right things. We will focus on the right things if when we choose what to do, we are in a good state of mind to do so — not fatigued, or distracted, or distressed. We will then attend to more of what we want and need to undertake in our lives. If, instead, we aimlessly tumble into situations, we'll attend to much less of what matters.

Timeboxing helps us get through most kinds of tasks. Urgent tasks with imminent deadlines are identified and prioritized easily through timeboxing. Non-urgent activities, such as learning, are also addressed, by being assigned specific timeboxes, when the time is right, rather than forever being canned and kicked down the road. Hard tasks, often avoided consciously or subconsciously, are instead met head-on at the times we are more likely to have the strength to carry them out. Easy tasks — which individually may seem too trivial to make a plan for — can be batched together into a single timebox of worthwhile size and substance. Useless, counterproductive tasks are shown up for what they are: undeserving of a place in our calendar, and we are apt and right to dismiss them.

Let's try to quantify the benefit here as well. Suppose that the value of a task is rated on a scale of 1 to 10. And suppose that when you work on tasks just as they come, the average value is 6. Suppose further that when you choose tasks ahead of time, the average value is 8. Well, that's a 33% uplift in value. That uplift may be much greater if we assume that the 80/20 rule applies to knowledge work. A small number of vital tasks may well contribute the majority of its productive benefits.

Parkinson's so-called law

We can get more done by inverting an old adage. Parkinson's Law[29] is the tongue-in-cheek but widely held assertion that 'work expands to fill the time allotted for its completion'. If you have 30 minutes to tidy your room, it will take you that long; yet if you have 60 minutes available, it still takes 60 minutes. The loss of time described by Parkinson's Law is associated with and explained by procrastination. Timeboxing seizes on a flip side of the adage: work contracts to fill the time allotted for its completion. So, if you reduce the time allotted to a timebox, you'll get the same work done. Sounds like a bargain.

There are scientific studies that support the idea. In one study,[30] undergraduates were asked to judge four sets of photos. Just before the experiment began, one group was told that their fourth set was cancelled. Yet they took almost as long to complete the work as their peers who were judging four sets; the work of judging three sets of photos expanded to fill the time allotted for its completion: 'Whenever anticipated work on the next task is cancelled or, more generally, excess time arises, dalliance by workers on their present task could amount to substantial and costly inefficiency.' This effect was observed in several replications. In another study,[31] participants were randomly assigned either 5 or 15 minutes to complete identical tasks. Those given 15 minutes took considerably longer to finish the task. A third study[32] reported that more than one-third of the variation in final exam scores could be attributed to procrastination.

There are of course limits to the so-called law. You might set a limit of an hour to write a ten-thousand-word proposal from scratch, but you will fail. Timeboxing is not quite magic. The studies alluded to above generally claim time savings of a quarter to a half. There are also studies that suggest that quality is diminished as the allotted time is reduced. A more recent (2014) study[33] confirmed this: 'Students working under time pressure obtain an average grade of about 3 points lower than the grade achieved by students working in absence of time pressure.'

All of this seems plausible: both that we reduce the intensity of our efforts with a remote deadline and that we do so to a limited extent only. Still, if we can squeeze an extra one-third of output out of our time by knowing about this tendency, let's.

Getting it all done in time

Timeboxing breaks down large tasks into smaller, manageable tasks of predictable length. The method therefore enables you to see all the components of a chunky project (moving house, launching a new product, organizing a big birthday party). This helps you determine whether it can indeed be done in the time available (or whether you need to make an alternative arrangement). It also helps you to ensure, if there is enough time, that the component tasks all get done before the deadline.

Multitasking

We covered some of the negative emotional impacts of multitasking in Chapter 4. But multitasking also has a negative and quantifiable effect on productivity.

For most people today, multitasking is the attempt to simultaneously manage notifications (in any of their forms) while carrying out another task. No one really tries to write a report while having a conversation or rake through expenses while delivering a presentation. Modern software (Microsoft Teams, Slack, email, etc.) and hardware (laptops, tablets, smartphones, smartwatches, etc.) combine to deliver many dozens of notifications every day. These are not coordinated helpfully with our other tasks and work. So, the temptation to check who sent what is real, constant and hardwired.

We usually get more done by single-tasking. Multitasking and context switching *are* less productive: a 2001 paper showed that the cost to business of multitasking and context switching was as much as 40% of productive time.[34] Multitasking can even be dangerous in certain contexts, as in texting and driving — in the US, each year, over three thousand fatalities[35] result from distracted driving. And certain tasks, for which cognitive load is high (such as helping a child to understand algebra or reviewing a legal document) and resumption lags long, are especially vulnerable to interruptions and multitasking. Admittedly, there are some rare combinations of tasks that can reliably be carried out simultaneously, and we'll consider some of those in Chapter 18. But for the vast majority of activities, timeboxing triumphantly kiboshes the possibility of multitasking, declaring and enforcing the power of doing one thing at a time.

Pockets of time

We all get pockets of time over the course of our day. While we're waiting for a bus. On our commute. Waiting for a friend to meet us for coffee. Those blessed occasions when a meeting finishes early or gets cancelled. Most of us allow these pockets to get filled with some kind of screen activity. Reaching towards our phone is a recent, emergent default behaviour. We now spend more than 2 hours a day[36] on bite-sized social media content, consumed with near-perfect convenience on our smartphones. We scroll and scroll, often without even enjoyment; we're addicted, rather than entertained.[37] Our pockets of time are eaten up, to the benefit of Big Tech companies but not to ours. The lost minutes accumulate into hours and more. Imagine if we used some of this time for more worthwhile pursuits. Timeboxing and intentionally using these small, unexpected pockets of time as they occur might give you an extra hour of productive endeavour each day.

Bottomless pits

Knowledge work is endless. Some productivity experts suggest that the correct response to this fact is to accept it and turn away from it. Emails are often put forward as an example of this: you have lots of emails, you reply to them, so you get lots more back again and it's . . . endless.

This is not quite right. While we will probably never get to our last ever email (in this sense it really is endless), there is often much of value in the information exchanged via emails. Although you may return to an enlarged inbox after having sent some emails, in that time, your project may be closer to completion, that deal may have now been done, your team member may have felt more included — as a result of that flurry of emails. Of course, you also need to establish control over your inbox and not let it overwhelm you emotionally or unduly impinge on other responsibilities. There are ways of safeguarding against this that we will come to in *Chapter 11 — Box-making*.

If we consider all the compounding factors at play — working on the right things, squeezing the most out of each timebox, replacing multitasking with single-tasking and deriving value from seemingly endless pursuits — the productivity uplift will be

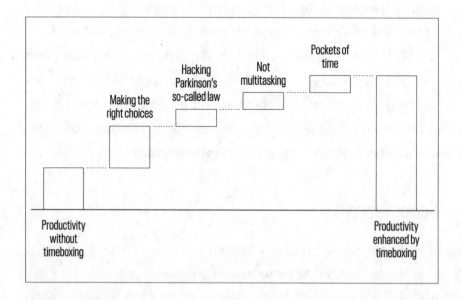

big. (Interestingly and coincidentally, dieters who measured and monitored their caloric/calorific intake achieved twice the weight loss of those that didn't.[38]) It may be naive to put a number on it, but it feels to me that timeboxing properly adhered to could well yield at least the doubling in productivity I suggested in my 2018 article.[39]

■ ■ ■ ■

As we add the benefits discussed in the previous three chapters — feeling better, thinking smarter, collaborating more harmoniously — you should be starting to recognize timeboxing as the super-power it is.

But even that's not all there is to it . . .

Review

- Achieving more with our time is a worthwhile pursuit.
- Timeboxing increases productivity chiefly by focusing us on the right activities.
- Parkinson's Law is backed by scientific studies; using it in our favour can increase productivity by one-third.
- Multitasking hampers productivity by up to 40%.
- Utilizing pockets of time through the day as you intend rather than as the algorithms in your apps dictate may bring you an extra hour a day.
- Overall, timeboxing will double our productivity.

Reflect

- How confident do you feel that you focus mostly on the right things? Are you more confident about that at work or at home?
- Do you multitask? In what situations? Do you feel you need to make a change there?
- Which is the biggest time thief of your life? Is it social media? Streaming services? Arguments? Other addictions? Worrying? Procrastination?

And as I hung up the phone, it occurred to me,
He'd grown up just like me,
My boy was just like me.

— Harry Chapin and Sandra Gaston Chapin, 'Cat's in the Cradle'

8. For an intentional life

Keywords	Life; purpose; meaning; planning; choose life; regret; intention; poignancy; cherish
Word count	1,524
Read time	8 mins

Time well spent renders a life well lived.

Timeboxing can improve your use of a 15-minute stretch, or an hour, or a day. These are the short-term durations usually associated with the method. But these periods add up over the weeks, months and years. And so it is that timeboxing can help you choose and change your whole life. That life might be all you can affect, all you will have, across the entire universe and for all eternity. In its very finitude — Oliver Burkeman's term for one vital aspect of the human condition — lies our great opportunity to choose what we do, and make our life special.

All the benefits we've explored so far combine to tell a complete story. Through timeboxing we feel better, think smarter, collaborate harmoniously and achieve more. These benefits intermingle and accrue. In the process, we leave a trail — the searchable log described in Chapter 3 — of all we have done. As we live through more of our lives, that trail grows. We ensure that the trail is rich and on our terms by proactively choosing our near- and long-term futures. Timeboxing helps us to do that.

The near term

Let's think of the near term as the next 12 months.

We are pulled in many different directions by many different areas of our lives. Timeboxing encourages us to think about these tensions, to settle them with an intentional aspiration and it helps us to realize that aspiration. This can be very tangible. For example, suppose you decide it's important that you spend more of your life on creative pursuits. Then think of some related creative activities, timebox them into your calendar and label them with a particular colour — say, blue.[40] Your calendar instantly becomes both a visualization of how you are doing with this goal and a prompt (when there's not much blue) for when you need to take remedial action. You might even choose to be very precise about this: I want to spend 25% of my time being creative, say. It's all recorded in your calendar for review and refinement (and comes with a level of automation if you use a feature like Google's Time Insights or Microsoft's Viva Insights in Outlook).

It's worth thinking about what the important areas of your life are. A review of your historic calendar will provide one important source of inspiration. Here's a list of common life tensions to help you get to those that make most sense in your life:

- **Work vs leisure.** This is the most common, the cliché. Still, it's important. What's a healthy number of hours for you to work, on average? Set them, do them and then down tools and work no more. You will need to take measures against the encroachment on leisure time by using devices and software (see *Chapter 23 — Tools & tech*).
- **Self-care vs responsibilities to others.** Do you spend enough time looking after yourself? Meditating, exercise, diet, journaling, therapy, reflection?
- **Learning vs work.** How much time do you spend learning during working hours? Does your employer

accommodate this? If not, perhaps they should; many employers offer an hour a week these days.

- **Work-related tensions: office vs working from home; night vs day shifts; challenging vs repetitive roles.** Have you thought carefully about what works for you, your family and work? If you have, have you done all you can to effect that change?

- **Social vs family vs alone.** Do you still spend as much time as you'd like, or as you should, with good friends? Do you even know who your truly good friends are? Do you spend enough *quality* time with family — for example, do you have family meals together and are you fully present when you do?

- **Productive vs leisure time.** Outside of work, we can still choose to be productive. Exercise, sports, musical instruments, reading, life admin and learning a new language are all considered productive. But do you spend *too* much time on such pursuits? Perhaps you need an injection of fun and frivolity? If so, how much and when? Timebox it!

- **Short-term goals (within 12 months) vs long-term goals (beyond a year).** Do you get the balance between the short and long term right? What is that balance, for you, as a percentage split?

- **Partner vs kids.** For those of us with both, do you spend the right amount of high-quality time with each member of your family? Is anyone a little neglected? Think about it, decide, and act on it.

The long term

Not so long ago, it made less sense to think about big, long-term life goals. We lived shorter lives and had a lot less choice. But now we live longer — in the UK, one in three of today's babies might expect to live to 100[41] — and, as argued in this book, we have a huge amount of choice, both of what we do at any given moment, and also of which life path to follow (where to live, whom to live with, what career to pursue, which skills to develop).

Life coaches often ask their clients in an early session to think up and write down their life goals. They offer prompts to help get to the stepping stones between the present and that future desired state. Timeboxing can provide those stepping stones and help us on our way.

When we near the end of our lives, most of us would like to be able to look back and feel that our time here was worthwhile and not experience major regret. It can be poignant and instructive, then, to consider some of the regrets that older people have expressed shortly before they passed on:

- spending too much time worrying[42]
- not saving enough money for retirement[43]
- not being true to themselves[44]
- not travelling more[45]
- not spending enough time with family and friends
- not pursuing their passions: many older people regret not pursuing their passions and dreams earlier in life
- not taking better care of their health
- not standing up for themselves
- not pursuing education or learning opportunities
- not expressing love and appreciation.

If you are moved to take pre-emptive action on any of these or some other regret, yet again, timeboxing can help. Suppose it's important to you to see more of the world. Think about when, where and what it would cost. Then make a plan. A monthly recurring travel-planning timebox would be a sensible start. Along with that, you might add some financial targets to help realize the goal. You then go on a trip or two this year and feel more confident that a similar (but improved) plan next year will also work out. And the year after that. A decade later, you will be the weather-worn wanderer you wanted to be.

An intentional, well-lived life needn't be glamorous. Much of what we do is commonplace and recurrent. We eat, drink, sleep, think and interact with those we live close to every day. Most of us could use reminders to eat a more varied diet, moderate alcohol consumption, ensure restful sleep, cultivate positive thoughts and extend kindness to others. Timeboxing can help us to do all of these everyday activities more healthily, intentionally and happily.

The long term can be seen to extend beyond our own lives. The ripple effects of our actions transcend our own existence. Certain positive or negative behaviours, especially those that affect younger people (including but not limited to our kids), are likely to live on in some form. We can choose to break bad cycles. And we can choose to initiate good ones. This is the warning and the opportunity spelled out by the lyrics at the start of this chapter.

The practice of intentional daily activity will eventually yield what almost every human being wants most: a chosen, cherished life.

■ ■ ■ ■

Over the past few chapters, we've reviewed the main benefits of timeboxing. Some help with the past (reliable record), some with the present (serenity, thinking smarter, collaboration and productivity) and some with the future (an intentional life). You may find it motivating to be able to visualize these all together:

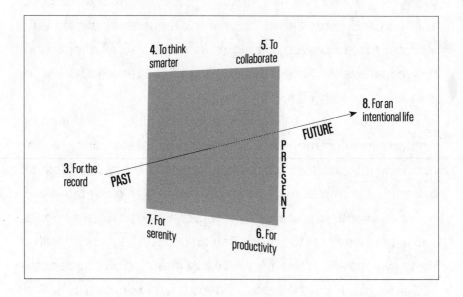

All we can be sure of, out of the entirety of the universe, is that we're here for a few decades, during which we get to make a few decisions. Let's use them to choose the life we really want.

Review

- How you spend your time each day adds up to how your life will have been.
- It's instructive to consider the current tensions in your life and whether your current efforts and time are spent in the right proportions.
- For the longer term, think about what life goals you

have, what milestones would lead to them, and what timeboxes in the immediate and near term will help you along that path.

Reflect

- Which of the near-term tensions listed in this chapter resonate most with you?
- What's one small change you could make that would improve one of the near-term tensions in your life?
- Which of the long-term life regrets listed above do you think you are likely to have, as things stand? What plan could you make to prevent that regret?

PART TWO — PLAN

■ ■ ■ ■

Part Two is about scheduling your timeboxes, before the hubbub of the day. As we saw in Chapter 2, implementation intentions work; that is, if you make a good plan, you are likely to see it through. Here's how to make one — with consistency, utilizing your to-do list, estimating how long each will take and ordering them appropriately. These essential 15 minutes of planning determine the following 15 hours of your day.

Do the best you can until you know better.
Then when you know better, do better.

— Maya Angelou

9. The basics

Keywords	Essentials; lay foundations; calendar; mindset; environment; workstation; distractions; focus; smartphone
Word count	1,235
Read time	6 mins

This chapter is easy-going. As we saw in Chapter 1, among other things, timeboxing is natural because we all already do it to some extent. Accordingly, very little is required to get going.

A little time: 15/15

Timebox timeboxing. This is not just a sound bite. One of the key ingredients of timeboxing, included explicitly in the definition in Chapter 1, is that we choose what to work on *when we are in a fit state to do so*. And that requires scheduling some time in the calendar before the tasks themselves, whether for daily time-boxing or the longer-term variety.

For daily timeboxing, this will most likely be the night before or the morning of your workday. The former holds the advantage of an extra night's sleep and whatever associations and consolidations your brain effects in that time. The latter has the benefits of fresh morning thinking (which I prefer).

You don't need much time. You can timebox your entire day in 15 minutes. But these are the vital few minutes that substantially determine the following 15 hours or so of your day. So, schedule those 15 minutes in your calendar. Note that this is a *daily* activity, very often your most important daily activity, so schedule it to recur each day. Make it appealing, especially at the start; for example, you might like to coincide your daily planning timebox with the sipping of your preferred morning drink.

These 15 minutes of planning bring control. Contrast this use of time with, say, jumping into your inbox first thing (which many people do). Suppose in those 15 minutes you made your way through ten emails. That's progress, of a sort, certainly. But it wouldn't give you a sense of how much you have on, your relative priorities, what most needs to be prepared for, who you need to drop a note to, when you'll be able to take a break, etc. Timeboxing gives you more than a sense of all this, it gives you a precise plan, and with it a feeling of control.

Longer-term timeboxing — weekly, monthly, quarterly or annual — should also be scheduled so you can be sure that it happens. You may need an hour or more for these longer-term planning sessions. But the focus of this chapter (and this book) is the most common and important cadence of timeboxing: daily.

Right mindset

For timeboxing to work for you, you'll need to be in the right frame of mind. You need to be open to the likelihood that the method can help you to figure out what you should do, when you should do it, and to feel better as a result of it. A critical eye is welcome and will actually help; steadfast cynicism will not. But since you're reading this book, you're likely to be of the mindset, i.e. of the view, that timeboxing can indeed help you. And since you've got this far, you will be aware of the six benefits of timeboxing laid out in Part One.

Right environment

Optimize your physical environment to get into and stay in the right headspace for your timebox. Treat each of your five senses in the way that's most conducive to clear thinking and good timeboxing.

- **Sight.** Turn off notifications, reduce access to notification-making devices and close the browser tabs you don't need (go full screen with F11 on a PC or Command + Control + F / Fn + F on a Mac). Make your calendar front and centre of your visual experience for this planning session. In the physical world, adjust the lighting, and keep your workstation neat and tidy. Take a few minutes at the end of this bullet point to consider the visual landscape from wherever you usually work or spend a lot of your time. Arranging our field of vision to avoid distractions is obvious but, in my experience, 95% of us don't do it.
- **Hearing.** Pick the right sounds for the occasion: music, no music, music without words, noise cancellation.
- **Smell.** Scented candles, diffusers, open windows, favourable aromas.
- **Taste.** Have any snacks and drinks that you want around; don't give yourself the constant excuse to escape from the task in hand to the kitchen/canteen/cafe.
- **Touch.** Get your posture right, surround yourself with the hardware and accessories that make you feel prepared, untroubled and focused.

Most people prefer to be alone as they timebox their day.

Deciding how you are going to spend your day is a personal activity. So, if you have your own room or office, shut the door and make people aware that now is not the time for chatter.

Our environments play a major role in habit formation. A list of all the items you need for your day (keys, wallet, phone, etc.) stuck to your front door may pre-empt unnecessary, irritating lapses. Leaving a book on your bed in the morning increases the chance you'll read it that night. Think about the usual physical and digital environment that you end or start your day with. What makes you feel motivated, good and focused? And what makes you feel unmotivated, bad and distracted? Surround yourself with more of what's good (see *Chapter 19 — Build the habit*).

A digital calendar

You really only need a calendar. Paper calendars (along with fancily designed pads of paper described by online retailers as timeboxing planners) are certainly compatible with timeboxing. But they lack many of the important benefits of their digital counterparts. Digital calendars can be mined for key information with a simple text search. Digital calendars are easily shared with colleagues, friends and family. Digital calendars can be protected with encryption and password protection. They are backed up in the cloud and synchronize across all your devices. The unequivocal advice here is to use a *digital* calendar.

There are some other, non-essential items that you can ignore for the time being. Many digital calendars come with advanced functionality, which very few of us use or need to use. Skip. There is also now software to help you timebox. Skip this too for now; we'll come back to it in *Chapter 23 — Tools & tech*.

Timebox timeboxing now

Go to your digital calendar now. Add a 15-minute appointment entitled 'Timebox today' for tomorrow morning, soon after you usually wake up, that fits with your life. Make the appointment recur every weekday. Then use them to timebox that day, and each day thereafter. This is an immersive, learn-by-doing experience.

■ ■ ■ ■

A quarter of an hour, the right mindset and environment and a digital calendar are all essential for timeboxing. But there's one more item we need to timebox properly. It's a very well-known and common practice, which has recently received (in my view unfair) criticism: the to-do list.

Review

- You need very little to start to plan your timeboxes.
- To get going, all you need is:
  - the right mindset
  - the right environment
  - a digital calendar
  - 15 minutes of planning time.

Reflect

- Look around your current working environment at the office or home. What good behaviours does it encourage? What undesirable behaviours does it encourage?

- When does it make most sense in your life to place your daily 15-minute planning timeboxes? What's stopping you from doing that right now?
- If you don't have a digital calendar, set one up, now. If you do have one, experiment with the settings to enhance your experience of using it.

Update list.
One thing.
Another thing.
Not all of these.

— Anon.

10. The to-do list

Keywords	To-do; list; reminder; prioritize; memory aid
Word count	2,643
Read time	13 mins

This is one of the most important chapters of the book.

The to-do list is a personal compilation of tasks that you intend to accomplish, often used as a memory aid. The calendar is a tool for keeping track of the events you have planned. Timeboxing is a coalescence of the two; it's taking the right items from your to-do list, placing them in the calendar and making sure they get done according to that schedule. To-do lists and calendars might have been two prequels to this book.

More than three-quarters[46] of us maintain a to-do list. But I suspect that very few do so optimally. To-do lists are almost always private, therefore it's hard to see what others are doing, share good practice, iterate or measure effectiveness. The literature (on the web and in books) on this subject reflects this; it lacks robust research and thinking and sounds flimsy and unconvincing.

This longer chapter establishes that to-do lists are indeed essential, describes what they are, where they come from and where they go, and helps you to do them better.

In defence of . . .

To-do lists seem to be out of favour. The main criticisms tend to be that they are one or more of:

- **Unmanageable.** We have so many things to do from disparate, incomparable areas of our lives and so the to-do list becomes unwieldy, overwhelming, impossible and even, according to Cal Newport (author of *Deep Work*), 'inhumane'. They therefore lead to stress and frustration and we make little progress on anything.
- **Unrealistic.** To-do lists set us unrealistic expectations of ourselves. We therefore burn out and/or feel like we've failed. A frequently cited statistic is that 41%[47] of to-do items are never completed.
- **Unambitious.** To-do lists focus on piecemeal, urgent tasks rather than contributing to bigger, broader life goals and values.

But these objections are merely objections to maintaining to-do lists *badly*. Knives, vehicles, words and countless other human inventions can be used ineffectively, poorly and even for ill. But what's at fault is the *application* of the invention, not the invention itself. We will see in this chapter that to-do lists done well rebut all the objections above.

In celebration of . . .

The to-do list is not just defensible, it's indispensable.

It's the list of items you deem important. Your agenda, your choices, your agency. This contrasts starkly with, say, an inbox, which is a list of messages and requests from others.

Its most basic function is as an aide-memoire. In these frazzled, frenetic times, the next thought, message, notification or experience is constantly chasing out the previous one. We're highly vulnerable to forgetting; in fact, it may even be an evolutionary design feature.[48] Simple, easily accessible to-do lists make sure we remember. The to-do list is also a respite for our working memory. By shifting an idea from a place where cognitive effort is involved to a place where it is not, our minds are unburdened, our stress eased.

It's also a manifestation of our potential. We are curating from the myriad ideas, activities and aspirations available to us as a free spirit on Planet Earth. It's drawn from your *could*-do list, which is bursting and shining with near-infinite possibility. It defines our ambition and capability.

The to-do list is an essential part of work and life for most people.

But although it's necessary, it's not sufficient for getting things done satisfactorily. The to-do list determines what we should probably do *at some point*. Timeboxing fixes those points and makes sure they happen as the future unfurls.

What feeds a to-do list?

Since to-do lists are, then, a prerequisite for timeboxing, we should understand them well. Let's follow the causal chain and ask: where do the items on a to-do list come from? There are five main sources:

- **Ideas.** You remember a promise you made to someone last week. A bright idea occurs to you in the shower. You see someone on the train who resembles an old school friend and it strikes you that you should be in touch with that friend. A creative, potentially useful thought comes to you from within a daydream. Our brains are constantly active and largely unpredictable. External prompts in our environment are also hugely unpredictable. So, the ideas, thoughts, occurrences and epiphanies that we have form one rich and fabulous source of ideas for what we might do. I advise keeping a to-learn list as a subset of your to-do list, to include anything you're curious about but may not have had the time to act on just when that curiosity was sparked.

- **Messages.** We receive over a hundred[49] emails a day. We get a similar total number of messages through messaging and social media apps. Many of these are mere automations, FYIs, unsolicited and irrelevant or otherwise trivially ignorable. But some of them require some level of thought and corresponding action and they become a thing-to-do, a candidate for your to-do list. Even the trivial many need to be dealt with somehow, and this also becomes a thing-to-do.
- **Meetings and conversations.** We spend a quarter of our working lives in meetings. We have 27 conversations[50] each day. These real-time interactions with other human beings can give rise to tasks in many ways. A boss can simply assign you a task. You get chatting to an elderly neighbour and offer to help fix their fence. Some of the actions that come at the end of a business meeting may have your name assigned to them.
- **Work itself.** As we finish the sales deck, we realize we'll need to rehearse it. As we write the business case, we realize we'll need to conduct more research into that addressable market. As we use the Customer Relationship Management (CRM) software, we realize there are several entries that need filling out. As we log

into our task management software, a series of tasks awaits us. Work begets work.

- **Life chores.** There's a lot of personal admin: laundry; cleaning; shopping; paying bills; cooking; maintaining a car, house, garden or allotment; exercise; personal health; planning holidays; caring for family and pets; taking out the rubbish and recycling; community responsibilities, and so on. Many of these recur regularly, some are less predictable. Some will come from family members, especially those we live with. All are tasks to do, and whether we enjoy doing them or not, they need to be done.

Recognizing the main sources of tasks (you will likely be able to add to the list above — can you?) and adjusting how they reach

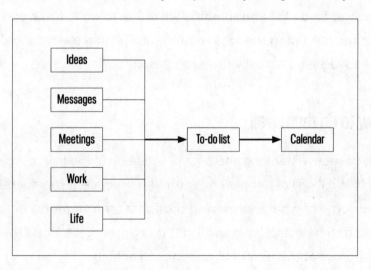

your to-do list can be transformational. For many people, there is a break in the chain between the source of the task and their to-do list. That means that items will sometimes get lost and never get done. Occasionally, this will be an important omission with costly consequences, at work or domestically. If you don't want to miss anything, you can't afford a break in the chain. You can only ensure an unbroken chain by looking all the way along it, right back up to the beginning.

What does a to-do list feed?

The to-do list feeds your calendar, your timeboxes. When you come to plan your timeboxes (with a little time, a digital calendar, and the right mindset and environment), you'll need the material for the timeboxes and this will come from your to-do list. And in feeding your timeboxes, as you go through your day, as the tasks get done, your *done* list is also effectively taken care of, for free.

Your to-do list should also feed your trash! Not all of our ideas are good. And, indeed, between the time that the idea makes it onto the to-do list and the time we come to do it, the world can change, rendering the idea redundant. Getting everything done on a to-do list is actually the wrong aspiration.

How to do them well

The collective thinking and best practice on to-do lists, considering that billions of people engage in the practice, is mediocre. I've read some of what there is and brought some elements of timeboxing to bear and have written this chapter in the hope that we all improve at this essential, overlooked activity.

Manageable units

Break tasks down into manageable chunks. Of course, what is manageable to one person may not be to another, but the consensus (with which I agree) is that tasks should be less than half a day and, ideally, a couple of hours long at most. But they could also be miniscule, e.g. a reminder to send a chaser email or to buy some milk on the way home. Bear in mind that the next stage in the process, timeboxing, provides an opportunity to break tasks down further or bundle them together. We don't need to do all the disaggregation right away.

For each task, write down enough details that you'll remember what it's about when you return to the list ('Research astral projection' works; 'Research', on its own, may not a few hours or days later). Additional information — estimated duration, importance, urgency, dependencies, collaborators, deadlines, ultimate purpose, category — may also be useful, but not essential.

Process

Establish the categories of feeds (see above) and systemize this in a way that aligns with what you deem most important in your life. For example, 1.2 billion of us use WeChat, two billion use Whats-App and five billion send and receive SMS messages. Unless you're happy to forget to fulfil promises and undertake tasks, you'll need a system for when a chat message should become a task. For example, star or bookmark messages that require action and set a (possibly recurring) timebox for when to address such messages. The point is to establish a flow from this category of task-generating activity through to your to-do list (and, in turn, to your timebox) — no breaks in the chain.

Establish an equivalent system for all the other task-generating activities that might feed a to-do list. Don't trust your memory, because it will sometimes fail you and, when it does, that frustration can be excruciating.

Some people operate multiple to-do lists. Those might be: work, social, financial, home maintenance, family, personal. For most of us that's counterproductive. It requires us to somehow make comparisons of importance/urgency of tasks across multiple lists in different places. Ultimately, each of us is a single entity with a single timeline. So, a single but all-inclusive to-do list should be sufficient, especially if we're discerning about what makes it there.

Start with a verb, because a verb is a *doing* word.

Sort it and keep it sorted (ordered by importance). This is the most important instruction and opinions are divided on how to go about this. One camp (including Cal Newport) advocates grouping similar tasks together, tackling them in those batches and inserting breaks in between in order for the cognitive context to dissipate in time for the next batch. That makes plenty of sense, but it suffers the disadvantage that urgent tasks may not be addressed soon enough (they're buried in bigger bundles). Another camp (to which I belong) advocates sorting by urgency or importance. One method (a very simple algorithm) here, when you are choosing from a long list of possible tasks, is to:

- Paste them into a spreadsheet.
- Assign each of them an approximate numeric value (1—10, say), denoting its urgency/importance in an adjacent column.
- Sort them by the numeric values in that column.
- Focus your attention on the crucial few items at the top (the peripheral items will be at the bottom).
- Enjoy a soothing sense of relief as a large, bothersome number of items of variable/unknown importance has

been transformed into a short list of must-dos.

- Treat the long list of unimportant items appropriately.
  Either delete them or schedule some time in the future
  to review them again (by which point some may have
  gained in consequence).

So, think about which way of sorting tasks makes more sense to you but be sure to sort, somehow. Without an ordering that you believe in, you're constantly second-guessing yourself, looking down the list, wondering whether another task should take precedence. An ordered list removes that anxiety-laden burden of choice and is yet another manifestation of the power of doing one thing at a time.

Prune it ruthlessly and regularly (pruning to-do lists is itself a timeboxable task and works well as a recurring calendar appointment). Feeding the trash with jettisoned items from your to-do list (i.e. crossing out or deleting them from the to-do list) is a healthy part of the process.

Note that there are many pre-made to-do lists, easily found online, which may be helpful to you: travel, camping, interesting conversations, shopping, home cleaning, moving home, interview preparation, home safety, home improvement, bucket lists and so on. Utilize the good thinking and shared best practice of others. Or ask a generative AI to produce you a list.

Mechanism

I maintain that a to-do list is happiest in digital format and in the cloud. That way, it can be hyperlinked, shared, copied and pasted and backed-up more easily (these are many of the same advantages enjoyed by users of a digital calendar). You certainly want to be able to rapidly access the list, wherever it is. You can't have ideas dissipate between the having of the thought and the jotting it down; friction must be minimized.

Personally, I use a single Google Doc for all my notes as well as my to-do list items. When I feel bewildered by the number of items I have (e.g. on returning from a holiday), I paste the to-do list into a spreadsheet, assign values, sort and timebox, as described above.

Dream big

Many of our to-do list items will be mundane. Most of the examples given in this chapter so far have been. But limit your to-do list like this and you limit your life. A dream can feel remote and unattainable, but it may just be a to-do list entry and a few carefully placed timeboxes away. Whether you want to learn a new language, switch careers, campaign for a cause or become a kinder person, there will be a small first step you could take, for which your to-do list could be a happy (temporary) home.

■ ■ ■ ■

The to-do list is there to help, not hinder. Don't overthink it, don't overcomplicate it. If you try to record every detail and adhere to arbitrary limits (a minimum of X big tasks per day, a maximum of Y tasks on your list, etc.) that some productivity guru made up, you'll be less likely to keep to this important habit. What's truly essential from this chapter is that you take a look at what feeds your list, that you sort that list somehow and, of course, that you then use it to timebox.

Review

- The to-do list is an essential ingredient to timeboxing and most people keep one.
- Ideas, messages, meetings, work and life and more feed to-do lists.
- Items from the to-do list migrate to a timebox in your calendar (and your trash).
- Good practice includes:
  - breaking them down into manageable chunks
  - keeping them prioritized
  - pruning them every so often
  - keeping them digitally and in the cloud
  - being ambitious.

Reflect

- Think about the categories of activities that feed your to-do list. Are there any more than those listed in this chapter? Which gives you the most work to do? Which do you enjoy?
- Could you improve your personal system of feeding your to-do list? How will you do that? *When* will you do it?
- Take a look at your current to-do list. How might you improve it right away, in the next 5 minutes?
- Do you know anyone who seems to never forget a thing? Ask them about how they compile and maintain their to-do list.

Wherefore that box?

— William Shakespeare (*The Winter's Tale*)

11. Box-making

Keywords	Bundle; batch; chunk; metadata; keywords; #hashtags; doing words; email
Word count	1,729
Read time	9 mins

So, we have our to-do list. More specifically, we have an ordered inventory of tasks of various sizes and a watertight system for keeping it updated.

We're now ready to make the corresponding timeboxes, to box-make. This chapter and the next two are all about creating and placing timeboxes and they are relatively straightforward. They should also be important since you are on the verge of making hundreds of thousands of timeboxes yourself (20 a day, 7,000 a year . . .) — what an extraordinary, empowering prospect!

Your objective when making a timebox is to facilitate a good, productive session when you come to the timebox itself: fast start, smooth progress, successful completion.

What kinds of things?

What kinds of things go into a timebox? Anything at all that you need or want to do that is of manageable size. They should come from your to-do list items, which as we saw in Chapter 10, originate, in turn, from your ideas, messages, meetings, work and life. To-do list items may require bundling (if they are small) or unbundling (if they are big).

Timeboxes usually represent one of:

- **The timebox planning session itself.** The approximately 15-minute period described in Chapter 9 in which you timebox the day ahead.
- **A task.** The activity you planned in your timeboxing session is the main use case, for example, taking the kids to the park, hanging out the washing, lunch with a girlfriend, writing the introduction to a report, reviewing that appraisal, revising the figures in the business plan, taking out the rubbish on Tuesday evening . . .
- **A reminder.** To contact that person, to chase that email, to buy that present . . .
- **Meeting prep.** Every meeting that goes ahead should be important. And every important meeting should be prepared for. A timely timebox is the perfect way to do this, either solo or in collaboration with other meeting-goers. Note that meeting prep will often be prompted by certain calendar entries. You sit down to plan out Tuesday. You notice a meeting on Wednesday requires a little work. In goes a Tuesday prep timebox.
- **A commute.** If you need time to get somewhere, indicate in your calendar for which periods you will be in transit (and presumably less available). But also think about enriching that commute with some intentionally chosen (and additionally timeboxed) entertainment or education. The timebox titles of my commutes are usually of the form 'commute / [some activity]'.
- **A break or exercise.** Remind yourself to take breaks and exercise. Signal to others that you are thus occupied, and when.

- **A recurring meeting.** Lots of meetings are regular (and some for good reason). Setting recurring calendar appointments to denote this is logical and efficient. Don't deprioritize these just because the reminder is automated. And recurring meetings may engender a need for recurring *preparatory* meetings.
- **Personal items.** We have a work life and a non-work life. Yet however we divide them up, they need to fit within the single set of 24 hours we have each day. So, interweave timeboxes from all the areas of your life into a single calendar (see *Chapter 6 — To Collaborate*).

Bundling and unbundling

Some tasks are tiny. Putting the washing on, acknowledging an email or sending a thank-you text may take just a few seconds, but these tiny tasks can have an outsized impact on our lives. It often seems hard to justify the administrative hassle of assigning such tasks a timebox at all. This is solvable: bundle (or batch) these small items together into a more worthwhile cluster; name the timebox something like 'Various' or 'Misc'; get them done, together; and enjoy the resultant catharsis.

Email is an especially common case of this. Many productivity gurus advocate the designation of particular times of the day for checking and responding to emails so that the regular work schedule goes uninterrupted. Some emails require more concentration and focus, and these may warrant timeboxes of their own (and in these cases, to make for a useful log, it's worth giving them specific titles, rather than just 'Email'). For the rest, gamify the process by registering in your timebox how many emails you had before the session, notice how many you whittle this down to, and register that number in the timebox entry when you're done (such entries for me look like this: ✉emails [34] > [18]). Admin and personal items are also often good candidates for bundling.

Don't make the tasks too big

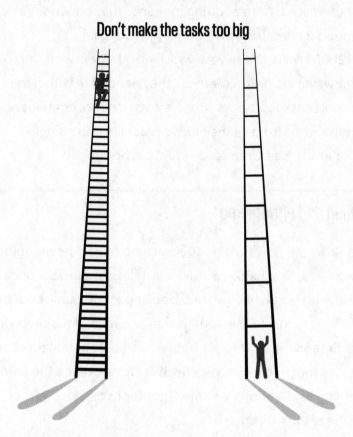

The opposite happens, too — a task can be too big. We find ourselves looking at something intimidatingly large (e.g. clear out garage, decorate house, write business plan, improve website) and we don't know where to start. Then break the big task down. Specifically, break it down into smaller units (see next chapter) and timebox these, not the big, whole thing. A good test of whether you've broken the task down sufficiently is if you know exactly what the very first thing you will be doing for each timebox is. For example, the timebox could be 'Vacuum the ground floor' and the first action might be to retrieve the hoover from the garage, or the timebox could be 'Invoice clients' and your first action might be to find the relevant invoices from your email.

Descriptors

You need very little information for a timebox. As with any agreed action, the essentials are a *Who*, a *When* and a *What*. The *Who* is, of course, you; it's your timebox, your calendar and your responsibility. The *When* we will get to in *Chapter 13 — Box-ordering*.

The *What* is the title and/or description, which needs to be sufficient for you to undertake that task effectively and without delay. With that end in mind, consider:

- **Naming (required).** This is important, particularly in the context of a shared calendar and collaborating with others. You want to see the name, know what it's about and ideally be primed and pumped to start the task. Pick a useful, evocative word: a technical term, the name of an event, a specific number that you will recognize. A verb will often work too and can bring some good, appropriate 'doing' energy. Useful verbs for timeboxes include:

> review, edit, email, write, read, summarize, call, think about, consider, brainstorm, code, plan, analyse, prepare, check, validate, ask, complete, improve, convince, respond, extend, increase, organize, plan, raise, build, consider, decide, develop, assess, reduce, consolidate, synthesize, watch, listen, help, understand, learn, find.

- **Description (optional).** You rarely need this. 'Jiujitsu class', 'Summarize 4pm meeting' or 'Improve LinkedIn profile' as titles may well be enough to get going. If more details are necessary, you don't necessarily need to spell them out in the timebox; a link or reference to the source information (a website, your notes, a document) is preferable.

- **Colour-coding (optional).** In Chapter 8, we saw that timeboxing can steer you towards greater, more intentional life goals. By colour-coding different kinds of activities, you can monitor how much time you're spending on each at a glance, by day or week or month, and decide whether and how to adjust those proportions. My timeboxes fall into one of four categories:
  - Blue — regular work
  - Green — high-value work
  - Yellow — leisure
  - Purple — writing

Google Calendar recently made this kind of analysis a lot easier with their Time Insights feature.

- **Hashtags (optional).** In Chapter 3, we saw that timeboxing can serve as a system of record. If you are meticulous and consistent with your naming conventions, you can make this work well. By using a personal taxonomy of useful terms, you will be able to bring up all your #1–1, #salesopp, #overtime, #projectX timeboxes with a simple search in your digital calendar.

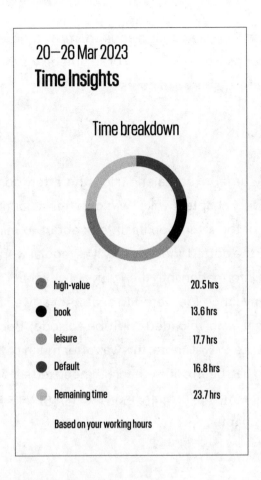

20 – 26 Mar 2023
Time Insights

Time breakdown

high-value	20.5 hrs
book	13.6 hrs
leisure	17.7 hrs
Default	16.8 hrs
Remaining time	23.7 hrs

Based on your working hours

- **Emojis (optional, obviously).** This will sound absurd to many but resonate with a few. Adding an emoji at the start of the timebox can lift the mood in which you go into that timebox. For those who heartily go forth in this direction, use sparingly for maximum, sustainable impact. I will confess, I do this, sporadically (🫖 for thinking, 🥐 for commuting, 🐕 for dog walks, ⚓ for getting kids ready, ⏳ when emphasizing the importance of a pre-eminent time management method).

Given how little is actually required, most timeboxes can be made in seconds. So, your twenty or so timeboxes for the day can easily be made in 15 or so minutes.

Examples

Below is my timeboxed calendar on the afternoon that I first drafted this very chapter (while I was on a transatlantic flight). The timeboxing of the afternoon itself took about 10 minutes and is indicated by the dotted line (I classify it as regular work). I then put just enough information into the 13:45 activity that I'd know how I'd receive my lunch (delivered to seat 45C) as well as my audio entertainment (a downloaded YouTube episode). Because I knew the material pretty well (note: this was after much of the research and planning had been done in earlier timeboxed sessions), single-word titles (at 14:15, 14:30, 14:45, 15:15 and 15:45) were sufficient for drafting the chapter.

■ ■ ■ ■

Though they are quick to create, timeboxes are themselves pieces of work to take pride in. Indeed, if you use a shared calendar, your timeboxed calendar may well be seen by others. But even if it isn't, this is your system of personal productivity. The better the timeboxes, the better their output.

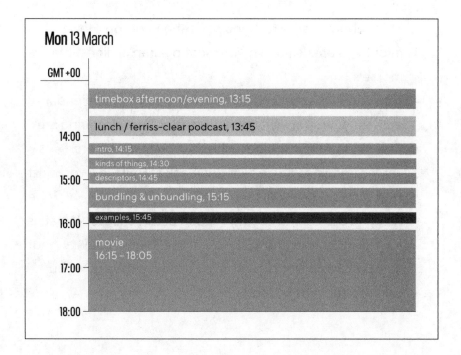

Review

- Timeboxes can be used for many different purposes. There are fundamentally two kinds of timeboxes: before-the-day planning timeboxes (15 or 30 minutes) and timeboxes through the day that describe the tasks themselves.
- Make sure the tasks you select to timebox are the right size: neither off-puttingly large, nor uselessly small.
- Describe them well, with active verbs and/or appropriate information. The title is key.

Reflect

- What kinds of tasks do you tend to shy away from? What characteristics do they share?

- Think about a large task you have ahead of you. How might you break it down into more palatable, digestible morsels?
- Take a look at your to-do list or your timeboxed calendar entries. How informative are your titles? How inspiring are they? How might you describe them with a bit more verve? Imagine yourself looking back at them in 6- or 12-months' time — will they make sense?
- Re-read the colour-coding section of this chapter. What are the most important (choose three, four or five) components of your life? Do you have any idea how you split your time between them?

One never notices what has been done;
one can only see what remains to be done.

— Marie Curie

12. Box-sizing

Keywords	Estimation; practice; empirical data; sampling; extrapolation; sense of time; paradox of choice; less is more
Word count	1,355
Read time	7 mins

How are we supposed to know how long a task is going to take? How do we estimate the time to allocate a timeboxed task? This is one of the most commonly raised concerns about timeboxing.

How much time will it take to reply to that difficult email? Or to change all the bed sheets in the house? Or to have that difficult conversation with your brother-in-law? Or to reformat that slide deck? Or to analyse last month's sales figures?

We need to be able to estimate how long a task will take — to box-size — for timeboxing to get off the ground. This is easier than it may at first seem.

Estimating doesn't seem easy . . .

There isn't much middle ground. If we underestimate our time-boxes, we won't complete the work or we'll do it poorly and feel frustrated and dissatisfied. If we overestimate them, we'll waste time and be unproductive. And for more involved projects that will be made up of multiple, cumulative timeboxes (painting the whole house, preparing for a violin exam, building a website), inaccurate estimation may have material, cumulative consequences.

Furthermore, many of us are prone to a cognitive bias, which encourages us to underestimate the time required for tasks. The planning fallacy — described by Daniel Kahneman and Amos Tversky in 1977[51] — is 'the tendency to underestimate the amount of time needed to complete a future task, due in part to the reliance on overly optimistic performance scenarios'. It's straightforward to take into account the steps involved in a task but we struggle to imagine setbacks — a phone rings, a server crashes, an unanticipated task emerges from within a task, a visitor knocks, a blizzard descends...

Somehow, we need to strike in Goldilocks' just-right zone. But how?

... but it's actually not that hard

It's perfectly possible to estimate the size of your tasks with a level of accuracy that makes timeboxing work.

For the vast majority of the things we do, we have some relevant experience to draw on. By comparing tasks scheduled for the future against similar tasks from the past, we effectively factor in the possibility and probability of unforeseen setbacks, as we have already lived through them in the gnarly, setback-laden real world. We have lived experiences of long, difficult emails, dirty bed sheets, difficult conversations, unruly slide deck, and raw sales figures, and how long they have taken to deal with. Of course, it's rarely *exactly* the same task that we're faced with, but near enough is good enough to timebox effectively.

Develop your sense of time

We can fortify our general sense of how long tasks take with explicit empirical data. On average, we: read 250 words a minute; process approximately one email every minute; take 3 hours to write 2,000 words; take 4 minutes to empty a dishwasher; take just 15 minutes to timebox the whole day ahead; 30 minutes to cook one of *Jamie's 30-Minute Meals*.[52]

We can make this more specific and pertinent by timing some of the activities we carry out personally. How long does it take you to:

- complete your usual jog/run
- do the laundry
- take a shower
- walk the dog
- get the kids ready for school
- research/write/edit a blog post
- prepare for a meeting
- approach five sales prospects
- clear an inbox of 50 emails
- write up notes from a meeting.

Seeing your common daily activities with timings laid out against each can be revelatory. You may decide to eliminate one of them or try to speed up a particular task or merge two, reasonably synchronized activities together (making a cup of coffee + emptying the dishwasher or listening to a podcast + going for a run). You might be surprised at how quickly some forbidding tasks can be done; and this may make them seem less forbidding. Laying out tasks and timings in this way will enable you to become better at estimating the size of your timeboxes.

When we really are unsure of a task, sampling may help. Suppose you have to review the CVs of 80 candidates and that you really haven't carried out a task like this before. Rather than box an arbitrary amount of time and likely get it wrong, you could review a handful of CVs, time how long that takes and extrapolate. For example, if 5 CVs take you 15 minutes, that's 3 minutes per CV, but perhaps you'll get a little quicker with experience, so the run-rate might be 2.5 minutes per CV overall, i.e. 24 CVs per hour. You therefore know that you'll need just over 3 hours, so around 3.5 hours with a break or two.

All of this should contribute to you developing a gut feel for how long tasks take, your sense of time.

Small, medium and large

I recommend just picking three box sizes and sticking to them. Trying to decide between small, medium and large boxes is a lot easier than picking from a number of time periods. Avoid pangs of indecision (is this a 4- or a 7-minute task?) by giving yourself a small number of options. Incidentally, this is why the Fibonacci sequence (0, 1, 1, 2, 3, 5, 8, 13, 21, 34, etc. — where the next term in the sequence is the sum of the previous two) is used to esti-mate the size of tasks in software development; most numbers are removed so engineers and product managers are unburdened from an unnecessary abundance of choice.

As for which sizes you go for, there are a few factors to consider. If you struggle to concentrate for long periods, opt for smaller timebox sizes. If your work is naturally geared towards certain durations, take that steer. The defaults on your chosen calendar software could also be a practical, logistical reason to go with, say, 25 minutes over 20 minutes; you don't want to have the hassle of making multiple adjustments in your calendar each time you add a timebox.

My timeboxes are 15, 30 or 60 minutes — small, medium and

large. Smaller than 15 is too small to be worth timeboxing (the admin becomes laborious, off-putting and self-defeating) and so I batch such tiny tasks together to make up larger, worthwhile time-boxes (as per the previous chapter). I find that tasks that are likely to take longer than an hour feel onerous, so I prefer to break these down into smaller chunks. My default timebox is 30 minutes. Note that a Pomodoro is 25 minutes and that Google's and Microsoft's default calendar appointment lengths (at the time of writing) are 25 and 30 minutes, respectively. There's wisdom in this crowd and sense in this consensus.

■ ■ ■ ■

Just start. Your estimated timebox sizes won't be right straight away, so expect to make mistakes and adjust. If you overestimate or underestimate the size of some tasks early on, you can adapt the scope (e.g. speed up by cutting some corners or slow down by taking greater care), which is a core feature of timeboxing (see Chapter 16). Remember, the aim of a timebox is to get something done to a level of acceptable quality; that level can be dialled up or down. For most tasks, there's no objective fact about how long they should take. Flexibility is key, appropriate and necessary for box-sizing and timeboxing.

Review

- Estimating how long tasks should take is necessary for timeboxing, but it's not difficult.
- Guard against the planning fallacy — where we underestimate the delays that the unexpected can bring

- — by heeding real-world experience wherever you can.
- We can develop our sense of time by observing what we do and how long it takes.
- Pick a small, medium and large timebox size and stick to those. My specific recommendation is 15, 30 and 60 minutes.

Reflect

- List some activities that occur frequently in your life and estimate how long they take you.
- Now find a way to actually time these activities. Are there any surprises? What efficiencies could you make?
- How long will it take you to read the next chapter? Time it. How does that compare to the estimated reading time?

It takes as much energy to wish as it does to plan.

— Eleanor Roosevelt

13. Box-ordering

Keywords	Sequence; series; order; priority; energy; hanging over you; face the music
Word count	2,413
Read time	12 mins

You've selected your tasks, you've made the timeboxes and you've sized them. Where in your calendar should you now place them?

Of course, in the knotty, gnarly real world it's not quite as cut and dried as this. In reality, you might choose the task, describe it, size it, re-describe it, order it, re-order it, resize it, or some such chain of quick-fire iteration. Nevertheless, the question of *where* to place the timebox in the calendar will arise at some point, *usually* after the timebox has been made and sized.

You will already have a sense of which tasks to look at first if they've been prioritized within the to-do list. To-do list prioritization will often require a refresh: overnight, your boss chased you for a response; a new forecast for rain means you need to cancel an outdoor event; you've remembered that someone is depending on quick dispatch of an item further down the list, etc. Your to-do prioritization is just an approximation for the ordering of your timeboxes.

As more and more people are able to work flexibly (in terms of hours and location), we have more options for when we do what, i.e. where to place our timeboxes. There are four considerations for deciding the order of your timeboxes: pre-existing commitments, dependencies, psychology and energy.

Pre-existing commitments

First, there are the pre-existing commitments in your calendar, many of which are likely to be meetings. At first, you'll arrange your timeboxes around these incumbent appointments. Over the coming weeks, try to push against this dynamic by deciding when you'd like to place your timeboxes for intentional tasks, and arranging meetings outside of those periods. Of course, this won't always be possible (a fixed volunteering commitment, an inflexible client, a colleague in a different time zone, a 1—1 with a time-poor boss), but choosing when you do what you want to do is an important part of reclaiming agency and feeling in charge of work and life. So, let people know that you'd rather not have meetings on a Friday afternoon, say. And the most effective and efficient way to let them know is, of course, to box out that time in your calendar.

Dependencies

Most tasks are not isolated islands of endeavour; they are related to one another. That relationship often takes the form of a dependency: booking accommodation before the holiday, the meeting prep before the meeting, the research before the writing, the rehearsal before the pitch, the team consultation before the hire, the purchase of the gift before the birthday. And, of course, when there's a dependency and a notion of a prior and subsequent task, the ordering of our timeboxes must reflect that. There are several types of dependency.

Important decisions

High-stakes decisions are dependent on high-quality, relevant information. That information should include data as well as consultation with the right people. If you can, find a way to incorporate at least one night of restorative, consolidating sleep between the gathering of the information and the making of the decision. For example, suppose you're hiring for a pivotal role. You're down to two strong candidates and it's neck and neck. Collect the job descriptions, the evaluation criteria, interview assessments, portfolios of submitted work, online profiles, disseminate to all who need to see the information, and give everyone a night or two before they come together to discuss and decide. So, one prior timebox for the collection and dissemination of info; another, subsequent timebox for the decision-making forum.

Meeting preparation

Meetings are common. Preparation is therefore important, by virtue of their sheer volume if not their high stakes. The difference between someone coming to a business call having done even 5 minutes preparation for it versus someone who just shows up for the call is palpable. The prepared person is more likely to be familiar and comfortable with the names of all the other callers, know when the last meeting took place, say something about the actions from the last call, and have a clearer sense of what they're trying to achieve. People tend to be even less well-prepared for recurring meetings, which, after a little while, lose their lustre. But recurring meetings recur for a reason — and that reason is that there is a standing issue that demands the repeated attention of some group. Buck this unproductive, unhelpful tendency to disregard such meetings by placing a recurring timebox several hours or a day before the recurring event (this is especially effective with easily-and-often-forgotten annual events like birthdays and anniversaries). Being thoroughly prepared, consistently, for meetings, is a rare behaviour and you will stand out if you can adopt this habit by timeboxing for it. You will become a higher-performing, more-reliable colleague, friend, daughter, etc. Timeboxing systematically enables forethought.

Consider preparing for non-work meetings too. You've arranged to pop by and check in on your mother-in-law. You said you'd have a cup of tea with an elderly neighbour. You promised to spend time drawing with your 8-year-old daughter tonight. Have you prepared for *these* meetings? A 15-minute preparatory timebox during which you list out what might really capture the imagination of a loved one in your next interaction with them may be the very best thing you do all year. These opportunities are so transitory. Remind yourself of some of the life regrets expressed in *Chapter 8 — For an intentional life*.

Collaborative dependencies

Suppose someone needs something from you. Assuming it's a request you wish to fulfil, ask them when they need it by, timebox a slot between now and that deadline, and tell them it's timeboxed, and when. They will appreciate you for this. Or suppose you need something from someone. Specify when you need it and ask them *when* they intend to do it. This may seem uncomfortably direct, but it's actually a perfectly reasonable request to make and a means of achieving the network effects of collaborative timeboxing. You may not be able to influence your whole company but perhaps you can influence your whole family or your whole team.

Soft dependencies

Sometimes there's a link between two events or tasks but not a hard dependency. For example, it might be *slightly preferable*: to have had that 1—1 with your colleague before writing their review; to have your new running shoes arrive before you go to the gym; to have read that report on sustainability in retail before lunch with an environmentally conscious boss. In any such cases, you timebox the prior and subsequent events, much as though they were hard dependencies. The connections between information, events, people and tasks are rich and complex and this is what makes life interesting and timeboxing an art. By intentionally curating, preparing for and sequencing what you do, you become the rightful architect of your conscious experience.

Reminders

Try as I might, I cannot think of a better way to remember minor items, in time, than placing a timebox in the calendar. This applies especially to basic, non-critical undertakings, which might not otherwise happen at all. Suppose a good friend has a job interview this coming Friday and it occurs to you to wish him luck that morning. How do you make sure you do? You could hope to remember it, which will occasionally be successful. You could add it to your to-do list, but what if you don't get to the list before Friday? You could set an alarm on your phone, but this is an extra administrative task on top of calendar management.

Much better to simply place a small timebox in your calendar early on Friday. This will practically guarantee success, and hopefully, your kind conscientiousness imbues your friend with warmth and courage on a day of nerves. Timeboxing guarantees that the task gets your attention at just the right time (a to-do list merely ensures your attention *at some point*). Notice also that this kind of reminder is of an event (someone else's job interview in this case) that you're unlikely to need or want to timebox for yourself; there's a dependency on something *outside* of your calendar, outside your immediate world.

Self-imposed deadlines

A deadline is an essential component of a task. A task without a deadline is incomplete, like a meeting without an end time. That deadline must be clearly communicated in order to timebox properly; if we don't know the relative urgency, we can't sensibly order our timeboxes — we can't prioritize. Nevertheless, sometimes no urgency is specified. This is often the case for non-collaborative projects like reading, learning or playing with your kids. In such cases, you need to *impose* a constraint. How much and how frequently do you want this in your life? Then insert it into your calendar and into your life to the desired extent and with the desired frequency. Through timeboxing, that notoriously neglected class of tasks — the important but not urgent — finally gets the exposure and attention it deserves.

A timeboxed calendar offers the perfect, practical visualization of all these types of dependency. You can see the subsequent task (which tends to go into the calendar first, paradoxically) and determine whether there should be a prior task, and how long the interval between the two should be.

3 dependencies visualized

	Mon	Tues	Weds	Thurs	Fri
8:00	Meeting prep				
9:00		Meeting			
10:00	Buy gift				
11:00					Guillermo's appraisal
12:00					
13:00					
14:00					
15:00		1–1 with Guillermo			
16:00					
17:00			B'day party		
18:00					

Psychology

Many productivity hacks advocate doing the hard stuff early. Common phrases convey this idea: bite the bullet, pay the price upfront, eat that frog, scary hour, face the music (my favourite). But there is also the quick-wins approach, which is the exact opposite: build momentum with your day by first getting some small tasks done and under your belt.

Personally, I prefer to start with the big, hard or more daunting tasks. I like the feeling that my day is going to get easier and this way I carry any worry for the least time. The scientific evidence[53] is divided on this but, overall, is more favourable to this approach. So, consider these general arguments and studies, and decide which — hard early or hard later on — works best for you.

Energy

Your energy levels are also a factor. Indeed, some experts prefer to talk of the management of energy as opposed to the management of time.

A crude and clichéd but common way of thinking about energy levels is in terms of the early bird vs. night owl dichotomy. We each have our own circadian rhythms and our personal rates of hormone production and metabolism. Do you wake early? Are you up and running soon after? Do you thrive in the tranquillity (no noise, no calls, no notifications, no *prospect* of any notifications) of dawn? If so, your calendar will tend to fill up earlier and you should be better placed to do more earlier. And, of course, vice versa. But note that early birds enjoy some advantages. Night owls have a slightly higher mortality rate[54] and society is also more structured around early starts. So, if you feel like you can choose (and a good 80% of us can[55]), go early.

Energy is also about mood. Are you ready to roll up your sleeves, put your headphones on and plough through a pile of monotonous work? Or are you after something creative? Are you up for social interaction or would you rather have a low-key day? Understanding what kinds of work suit which kinds of energy level for you is the skill here — one that Steve Jobs apparently deemed important.[56] Certain activities — like exercising, meditating, getting fresh air, a cold shower, taking a break — can boost energy, at least for a while. So, consider placing energy-enhancing timeboxes strategically so you're galvanized just when you need to be. The flip side of that is to not place psychologically or emotionally difficult tasks when you're likely to feel drained, e.g. after a long meeting, a public-speaking occasion, a day of enforced home-schooling, etc.

It's possible and sometimes desirable to monitor and manipulate your energy levels. Keep yourself under close observation by checking in every so often. How am I feeling? Is my energy high or low? Is it increasing or decreasing? And then consider whether to effect a change: a drink (coffee, tea, water), meditation, breathing exercises, physical exercise, a break, a walk.

Et voilà!

Your initial training to create a fully timeboxed day is now complete. On the day I wrote the first draft of this chapter, my own fully timeboxed calendar looked like this:

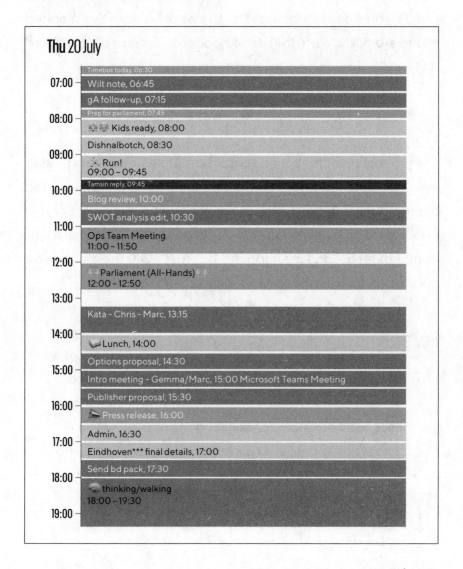

Some people are horrified when they see a fully loaded timebox for the first time. They call it a nightmare. In fact, a fully loaded timebox is not the nightmare; it's the only escape from the nightmare. The above is a lot to do in a day (note that most of my days don't pack in quite so much). But at any given moment, there was just one, single thing to do. Herein lies the peace and power of doing one thing at a time.

And when you've made, sized and ordered your timeboxes for the day, take a moment. Look at the whole day you've planned ahead. Admire it. Note that if it all happens as you've planned (and it's likely to, now, remember), you'll have lived a good day.

■ ■ ■ ■

The order of your timeboxes is important. They should be arranged logically and take account of your own personality, psychology and energy. But don't sweat it too much either; a timebox is not cast in iron. For me, one or two timeboxes move over the course of a day, as priorities shift and life happens. But that's OK; the manoeuvre takes just a few seconds and it's all part of the process.

Review

- Once you've selected your tasks and sized them, you need to decide where to place them in your calendar.
- Four considerations for deciding the order in which timeboxes appear in a calendar are: pre-existing commitments, dependencies, psychology and energy.
- Timeboxes can be adjusted as priorities shift, but this should be the exception, not the rule.

Reflect

- Do you prefer to get hard work done early in the day or later on? Have you experimented with the alternative?
- Which do you understand least well — how to make, size or order a timebox?
- Think about a relative you love. What do they enjoy talking to you about? What do you most enjoy talking to them about? List five such topics, save them on your phone, and make a timebox to review those notes just before (note the dependency!) you next see that relative.

PART THREE — DO

■ ■ ■ ■

Part Three is about how to get the most out of the method, in the moments of each timebox. Get started, move quickly, produce something tangible, and stay mindfully focused on the task in hand even as a thousand distractions hammer at your door.

The story's about you.

— Horace

14. This very chapter

Keywords	Learn by doing; application; immerse; notice; observe
Word count	1,129
Read time	6 mins

Start the habit of timeboxing in earnest right now, in the next few seconds. But how? You're busy, reading a book. We can work with that.

You're going to timebox the reading of *Chapter 14 — This very chapter*. Though this is not a standard timebox (it may not have been drawn from your to-do list), it will offer enough of the experience to be worthwhile and reaffirm what you've learnt so far, breathing extra relevance into the chapters that follow.

First, as we've just seen over the past three chapters, you'll need to make, size and order your timebox. This chapter has 1,129 words and should take just 6 minutes to read. But because you might pause once or twice to reflect on what you're reading and there's an exercise in the middle of the chapter, let's make a 15-minute timebox. What time is it for you right now? OK, so then the timebox is 'Read Chapter 14', it starts right now, and it finishes in 15 minutes' time. Your timebox has just been made, sized and ordered; planning is complete. You are now ready to step over an important, hypothetical line, and into the timebox itself.

So, now you are in it. In the timebox. You are timeboxing. You have therefore just succeeded with one of your aims in choosing this book, as have I, in writing it.

Cast everything else aside. It's critical that you stay focused on the remaining pages of this chapter for the next few minutes.

You are part of the story now

The Never-Ending Story, *Infinite Jest*, *If on a Winter's Night a Traveller*, the choose-your-own-adventure literary genre, and other imaginative works of film and fiction explicitly weave their reader into the narrative to beguile and entertain. At the least, I hope you are engaged.

Learn by doing

I'm taking an immersive approach in this chapter because we learn more by doing than by learning. More precisely, we learn best by interweaving theory with practice.

In the world of adult education, there's a theory of learning called 70:20:10. It asserts that 70% of our learning comes from job-related experiences, 20% from interactions with colleagues, and 10% from formal training. The numbers aren't precise, aren't intended to be, and don't really matter; what matters is the widely held belief that it's in the *application of the theory* that much (indeed, most) of the neural rewiring happens in our brains.

So, timebox; don't just read about timeboxing. This experiential undercurrent and encouragement should be familiar by now.

Small timeboxes to begin with

Well, we have started small. This is just one, short chapter to read and you're already one-third of the way through it.

For the next few timeboxes that you do, after this one, I suggest keeping the tasks similarly manageable. Have a think now — yes, while you are still in this Chapter 14 timebox — about what those next, modest timeboxes might be. Some ideas:

- Do you have a few niggling tasks that might be bundled up into a single 15-minute timebox? What are they? Make them happen. Move them to the top of your to-do list, now. Better still, make the timebox in which you will get those niggles addressed.
- Do you have any important meetings coming up in the next week? Pick one and make a 15- or 30-minute timebox before it in which to prepare. Or bestow on yourself a gift that will keep on giving: find an important *recurring* meeting and add a *recurring* timeboxed appointment a little before that.
- How about timeboxing an entire afternoon? Suppose it's Tuesday morning now and your Thursday afternoon looks relatively free. So, right now, timebox some tasks to fill that afternoon. And maybe that could become a routine itself — timeboxing Thursday afternoons the Tuesday before. Then set that Tuesday activity up as a weekly recurring appointment.
- Or set yourself a week-long challenge. Plan and commit to some timeboxes every day for a week. It could be to read the remaining ten chapters of this book. Could you extend the challenge to a month?

However you choose to start timeboxing, pause reading now, review your to-do list, and take a few minutes to add some small timeboxes to your calendar before carrying on with the rest of this chapter.

What do you notice?

If the timeboxing of this chapter is going to plan, you will probably have considered your role as the protagonist, accepted the idea of learning by doing, put the book down, added a timebox to your calendar, picked the book back up, and still have around 5 minutes left of this timebox. If that's exactly what's happening, congratulations, you're lucky, a natural.

And if it's not, you're also in luck: you have perfect material to contemplate. What was it that led you astray? Try to follow the chain. For example, did you get distracted? By what? Was it an external distraction or an inner thought? Are you sure it was exactly that? Or had you lost your concentration earlier still? Could the distraction have been avoided? How might you avoid it in the future? We'll burrow further into this warren of ideas in *Chapter 18 — Rabbit holes & other distractions*.

■ ■ ■ ■

You are now coming to the end of your timebox. Take a deep breath and slowly bring your awareness back to your surroundings and the other responsibilities of your day. Acknowledge the benefits of the practice and carry this sense of calm, clarity and productivity with you throughout your day. Remember that you can always return to this state of pragmatic peace and productivity whenever you need to. Thank yourself for deciding to use this time with intention.

Well done. Naturally, you will get better with practice and as you read more about how to do and to embed and own timeboxing for yourself. From the experience you've gained in the last 15 or so minutes, each page that follows should resonate more.

Review

- The chapter offers and is a timeboxing exercise for you to practise while reading it.
- Timeboxing can be picked up fastest by interweaving theory with practice.
- You will start best by starting small.

Reflect

- Did you timebox this very chapter? If not, why not? And if not, what is the next (small) task that you *will* timebox?
- If you got at all distracted during the reading of this chapter (and 99% of readers will have been), use that distraction to answer the questions posed in the 'What do you notice?' section.
- Does the 'learning by doing' method espoused and invoked in this book work for you? If you resist it, why do you think that is? What adjustment might help you to get more from the next suggestion to timebox as you go?

*A whole is what has a beginning
and middle and end.*

— Aristotle

15. Start—middle—end

Keywords	Long middle; prompt; punctual; conscientious; anti-procrastination; small acts; flow state
Word count	1,185
Read time	6 mins

You should have timeboxed now, at least once. But how could you do it better? What is good timeboxing practice in the simplest and most straightforward terms?

Of course, the start of a timebox is not the start of the process. Before the allotted time for your timebox begins, you've already planned it and before that you may have given the task some thought when it was a fledgling idea, in your to-do list. The point is that you shouldn't, and won't, arrive at your timebox cold. The method and mindset of timeboxing encourage the kind of antecedent cognitive whirring that will help you execute the tasks you've planned with aplomb.

Take your experience as the protagonist of the last chapter into this one. Remember how you felt at the start, in the middle and at the end, and you will start to shape your own version of timeboxing for yourself.

Start

The points about getting your environment right from *Chapter 9 — The basics* apply equally here. Indeed, there's greater likelihood of being derailed implementing a longer, 'doing' timebox than a shorter (15-minute), planning one.

Start on time. Beginning badly can lead to several undesirable outcomes. You will have less time for the task, you may not meet the deadline and, even worse, you might be discouraged altogether from the practice of timeboxing. Of course, sometimes you will start late. But sometimes should mean more like one-in-ten, not one-in-two.

Having an awareness of your start (and end) times is handy. To that end, pick round, familiar units of time (quarter-past, half-past, on-the-hour, etc.) rather than, say, 7:03, 12:19, 16:43, etc., for which the sheer arithmetic adds substantive cognitive burden. Make it easy.

Procrastination pulls on the heels of the prompt start. Much has been written on this common condition, so I'll just offer one pragmatic suggestion here that works for me and many others. When faced with a task and feeling some procrastinatory inertia, identify the very smallest, first action you need to start the task. That might be to open a file, read a particular email or look up that unfamiliar term. It might be ludicrously minute, such as to pick up a pen! For me, this first, small task is very often going to my personal notes file (which happens to be a Google Doc, maintained for the entire calendar year) and writing down the bullet points that will soon collectively constitute the task. That first, tiny physical action — the firing of the right motor neurones — kick-starts a chain of physiological processes from which the actions will follow and which will get your task done. Here are some examples of procrastination-vanquishing quick-start actions:

Task	Quick-start actions
Wash the car	- fetch the bucket - untangle the hose - find the car wash detergent - get the car keys in order to reposition the car (shade is best, apparently)
Proof a blog	- re-open the message requesting this task - scan the article quickly and painlessly - search for that blog - message the author or marketing colleague that you've timeboxed it and when, and when your proof will be with them
Check some invoices	- open Microsoft Excel - open up the invoice you can locate most easily
Book a holiday	- draw up a list of possible destinations and share for comment with friends/family members - search Google for 'main categories of holiday'
Reply to a difficult email	- think about why that person may have sent it - open it up and reread it, though it's unpleasant - write down the three things you need to say in your reply

Don't question the legitimacy of your timebox. You've already had that debate with yourself when you planned it. And remember, much of that internal debate is your subconscious finding ways to rebel against this important, somewhat difficult yet necessary task. And that debate will never end: replace your chosen task with another and that too will be vulnerable to further displacement. It's much better, instead, to have a system that, over the long run, will get you doing the things you mostly need to do. In the words of the Philadelphia 76ers: trust the process.

Middle

Beware the long middle. If a task is dull or big or saps your energy, you're much less likely to get it done within your planned time-box. So, keep the middle short by keeping all your timeboxes short. Although I maintain 15-, 30- and 60-minute timeboxes, the last and largest of these is deployed only for rare occasions, when I know I need to knuckle down to a longer stretch of continuous, deep work.

Ideally, by the time you're in the middle of a task, you will have achieved a state of flow (Csíkszentmihályi's concept). The enigmatic and coveted psychological state of flow is subjective by definition and hard to pin down. But it's generally associated with high levels of concentration and control, a loss of self-awareness, an intrinsic sense of enjoyment and a distorted perception of time. Note, though, that the last of these characteristics does not imply a complete lack of awareness of time (which would be problematic for the practice of timeboxing). One can actually be in a state of flow and simultaneously aware of the time and of the importance of checking the time every so often. Time may feel different but can nonetheless be actively managed through a flow state.

End

End on time too. Not doing so leads to the same kinds of undesirable outcomes as not starting promptly. We'll look at some ways of speeding up when we need to in the next chapter.

Make it a good ending. As you successfully finish the task, develop a routine micro-celebration: tick off an item as done, recolour a timebox, add a check emoji (✅) to it, or simply admire your adhered-to, timeboxed calendar with satisfaction. A more material and social way to celebrate your efforts is to share the output with someone to whom it's useful, pass the baton of progress on and keep the collaborative hive buzzing.

■ ■ ■ ■

With a little practice, you'll be timeboxing well: at the start, at the end and in between.

Review

- The start of a timebox occurs well before the allotted timebox itself, in the earlier planning session.
- Start well: on time and with the right environment.
- When feeling the onset of procrastination, identify the tiniest first action you need to take to start the task.
- Don't question the legitimacy of your timebox. Just do it.
- Keep the middle of the timebox short by introducing more frequent goals.

- Aim to achieve a state of flow by not making things too easy or too hard.
- End on time and celebrate the successful completion of the task.

Reflect

- How good are you at getting going with a task? What hurdles hold you back? Can you do anything to remove them or reduce their effect?
- Think about when and how you get into a flow state. Which conditions are conducive to it for you? How might you make those conditions more common to your experience of work and life?
- What's an appropriate mini-celebration of a task, for you?

Time is of the essence.

— English and Welsh contract law

16. Pacing & racing

Keywords	The project triangle; cost, time, scope and quality; innovation; checkpoints
Word count	1,731
Read time	9 mins

I'd like to think you're pretty committed to timeboxing by now. We want it to work, both the planning and the doing. One problem is when we get behind schedule in the timebox — we run out of time for the task. This might be because something unexpected cropped up or the task was harder going than anticipated, or perhaps we just squandered the time. With some advance notice and a suitable contingency plan — both expounded here — this commonly held, commonly faced objection to timeboxing fades.

But first, recall Chapter 12 about box-sizing and how to develop that skill. Early on in your timeboxing journey, accurately estimating the size of timeboxes is not trivial. But nor is it all that hard: get going, iterate, build experience and you'll soon be estimating 80% of your timeboxes with the right balance of challenge and feasibility. This chapter is for the 20% of situations in which you find yourself behind.

Midway checkpoint

If you know the start and end times of your timebox, you should have an intuitive sense of progress.

But that won't always be enough. Set an explicit midway checkpoint. The midway point in *time* is clear and obvious, especially if you set rounded start and end times. And sometimes the halfway point of the task itself is also obvious (numbers of: words written, lines of data updated, shirts ironed, dumplings folded). But there are also many other kinds of tasks for which progress is not measured linearly: coming up with a new tag line for a brand; planning a holiday for a group of school friends; making progress with your personal-development plan. For these, you will need to rely on and develop a sense of what on-track looks and feels like. You might also redescribe the task in a more granular, numeric way in order to quantify the task at hand. The examples cited above might become, respectively: come up with six tag-line options; find ten reputable sources of holiday information; curate a learning pathway of five items.

Quality, cost, time and scope

So, you've checked in at the halfway point and you're behind. What should you do?

We can use a concept from the world of project management. The idea is that for any project (i.e. task), there's a balance to strike between quality, cost, time and scope. This is represented by the diagram below, called the project management triangle:

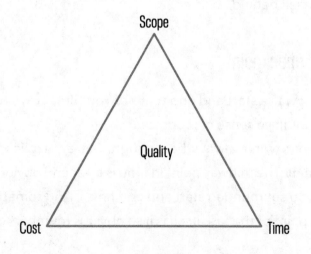

Trade-offs need to be made and good project management is about making the right ones, to the satisfaction of all those involved. It's a simple model and, in project management circles, is sometimes criticized for being too simplistic for the chaotic dynamics of the real world. But as a framework to analyse and help us through relatively straightforward, individual timeboxes, its simplicity is a blessing.

The triangle provides a structure to think about our options in the face of a time shortage. There are five options, and we'll use the example of dealing with cleaned clothes from a washing machine that's just finished its cycle.

Reduce quality

Aka speed up. Faster doesn't mean blind panic. We can be measured in our acceleration. Most often there's a graceful degradation to be found that strikes a practicable balance between quality and speed. *Hang up the clothes quickly so they dry but perhaps with more creases than you would like.*

Reduce scope

Aka do less. Some tasks have components that can be painlessly detached. In such cases, simply dispense with the most dispensable and finish on time, as planned. *Take out the items that you or your family most urgently need (in my household, this is always the Brazilian jiujitsu training uniform, the gi).*

Increase time

Aka extend the deadline. You need more time, so — assuming there's nothing mission critical on the other side of your timebox — give yourself some. It takes seconds to extend a box on a digital calendar by a few vertical pixels. *Take the extra 10 minutes you need to hang up the clothes properly.*

Increase cost

Aka enlist help. Timeboxing is a means of achieving personal productivity improvements where the only (albeit important) cost is the timeboxer's time. It's rare, therefore, that you will be able to get back on schedule by throwing money at the problem (by bringing in some external help, say). But it is conceivable and listed here for completeness. *Ask a family member to help you.*

Something new and special

Aka innovate. Refuse to sacrifice on any of quality, scope, time or cost; find a game-changing way of doing it (as the Fosbury Flop flipped the high jump on its head; Post-it notes became a new way to remember; barcodes revolutionized logistics; the iPhone changed everything). Less glamorously but more pragmatically, innovation might mean finding new software or an app or introducing a new Excel formula that makes a step change to your ability to carry out a task within the set time. This is the sweetest solution, so be minded towards it, but expect it to be the exception, rather than the rule. *Invest in a tumble dryer.*

In *Atomic Habits*, James Clear emphatically advocates reducing scope; indeed, one of his mantras is 'change the scope not the schedule'. He offers the example of reducing scope, from a 3-mile run to just 1 mile, when he has less time than planned. Other examples might include cooking a less impressive meal, vacuuming a single room rather than the whole of the house, or reading the single, seminal science paper on a topic rather than the five you had earmarked. In general, this is a useful, clarifying heuristic. But there are situations in which it makes more sense to reduce quality (speed up) or increase time (change the schedule). To add some imagined context to Clear's example: it's the weekend, you're at the start of a marathon training regime, and you have no external commitments that day. Here it probably makes more sense to give yourself a few extra minutes (i.e. increase time and change the schedule) than to curtail the run.

Context matters and the right solution to running short of time will depend on that context. And in the complex, composite real world, the best solution may be a combination of those listed above. One of the editing sessions of this part of the book serves as an example here. As you would expect, I had allocated a large box of time to review edits for these five chapters and made smaller timeboxes for each chapter, some of which were 15 minutes, some 30. At a certain point, I fell behind my schedule. I noticed this. I then had a few options: reduce the scope by reserving some chapters for another day or reduce quality by taking a less diligent approach to the work. Instead, I extended the timeboxes; this was one of those occasions where it felt most appropriate to flex time, rather than any of the other three parameters.

From chore to challenge

It's unfashionable and even frowned upon these days to advocate increasing the speed at which tasks are completed. People are frazzled enough as they are — we should be easing their burden, not piling on further pressure. I agree that mental health must be taken seriously and that burnout is a major contributor to it. Indeed, one of the chief benefits of timeboxing is to unfrazzle. But

I also believe that speed can be fun, especially when the time trial is a challenge we've set for ourselves.

A time limit and an implied need for speed can be a motivating factor. The chore of writing 100 words becomes more of a challenge if a realistic time limit (15 minutes, say) is placed on it. The countdown begins, a little adrenaline is released into the bloodstream, and there's a clear success/fail outcome at the end. You may have clocked that the time limit helps meet some of the conditions (in particular, matching the challenge with the skill, making it just difficult enough) specified by Csíkszentmihályi to achieve a state of flow. This is somewhat akin to the difference between being asked to describe yourself in an unlimited free-text box vs being asked to do so in exactly seven (say) words; people are more motivated and more likely to complete the second (harder) version of the task. For tasks you carry out repeatedly, you can establish a personal best to surpass: most words written in an hour; most emails processed in 30 minutes; fewest mistakes made in 15 minutes of data entry, and so on.

And if you can embrace speed and enjoy it, a happy by-product is, of course, increased productivity.

■ ■ ■ ■

If you have set your timeboxes up well, you generally won't need to intervene to get them done to an acceptable standard and on time. But when you are running behind, become aware that you are by setting a midway checkpoint; you need to know you have a problem in order to solve it. Then, if you are behind, be reassured that you have several options available to get back on track. Whichever option is right in your particular situation, understand that there is an enormous, underestimated benefit to sharing the fruits of your timeboxed labour with the world — aka to deliver, to share, to *ship something*.

Review

- For timeboxing to work, we need to keep to the scheduled timings.
- Sometimes we'll need to speed up.
- Success is partly predicated on estimating the size of our timeboxes well in the first place.
- Midway checkpoints help us meet deadlines.
- When we do get behind, we can: reduce quality, reduce scope, increase time, increase the cost or innovate radically. Reducing quality, scope and time, in particular, are by far the most common, pragmatic solutions in most situations.
- Setting a realistic time limit for a task can turn it from a chore into a challenge, which can be motivating.

Reflect

- Recall a situation in which you were running out of time to get something done. Which solution would have been more effective: scope, quality or time? And why?
- Do you know how long it takes you to read a page of a book? Time it, for the next chapter.
- Give yourself time limits for a variety of things you do today. Get more used to it and get better at it. When is this fun? When is it not?

Real artists ship.

— Steve Jobs

17. Ship something

Keywords	Deliver; share; ship; unveil; launch; satisfaction; good enough; usefully shareable
Word count	1,318
Read time	6 mins

You've done some work. Is it good enough? And how will it interact with and make a difference to the world? This chapter focuses on these two questions.

(A short note on *shipping*. The word in this context refers to the transport of goods that are available for use. Jobs was talking about computer hardware (specifically, the original Macintosh) in 1983, but the term can be used for any goods at all. More recently, this usage has become popular in software development, pertaining to the point when the product is released to end users. I use the term here to make the point that a task gains much value in its unveiling.)

Good enough = usefully shareable

In the previous chapter, we saw that there are several ways of adjusting the pace of productivity to get a task done. Of these, reducing scope, reducing quality and increasing time are the most common and important. Adding time needs little further comment here; if you need to, if you can, and if there's no better alternative, go ahead. But with scope and quality, how much can we sacrifice before our output becomes inadequate?

Perfection is neither necessary nor possible. Few need it and for many tasks, perfection (a perfectly arranged filing system, an immaculate kitchen surface, error-free grammar) might even go unnoticed by its audience. And human beings are rarely capable of it. So, let's all make a better plan and aim for good enough, even the perfectionists among us. But what does good enough look like, exactly?

A useful benchmark is whether it's ready to be shared. Shame and pride are powerful, ancient motivating emotions, which regulate our behaviour as social creatures. Accountability is a more contemporary concept that gets at the same thing. So, when we feel ready to share it, knowing that we have strong, deep-rooted aversions to ridicule, for most of us, it's probably good enough.

It also needs to be useful, meaning — though it's certainly not perfect — it is in some important sense *functionally complete*; it will work or the important aspects of it will be usefully understood by the recipient, the beneficiary of the task. To add a little more rigour to this, we can take an idea from product (not project) management. In product development, there's a concept of the Minimum Viable Product (MVP). This is the version of the product with the fewest features that will still be usable and useful to someone (in this case, beta users or early adopters). Being less mature and less sophisticated, it's relatively easy to put together, so the product team can observe how it's used and make improvements to the next version. The MVP is *usefully shareable*.

The idea of usefully shareable as a standard transfers to tasks generally. The structure of a business plan is usefully shareable; the first few paragraphs less so. An email confirming, possibly in a single word, the go-ahead for a project for an expectant team is usefully shareable; a detailed but inconclusive exposition of whys and wherefores is not. A bullet-pointed summary of your feedback on a colleague's poor PowerPoint presentation is usefully shareable; a brutal, thorough reworking of the worst slides in their deck is not (for multiple reasons). A roughly hung-up array of clothes to be distributed to select individuals is usefully shareable (someone else might then fold and distribute them); hanging up a random selection of clothes is not.

A lovely illustration of this point comes from a viral time-lapsed video of an artist drawing a picture of Spiderman.[57] In the first section of the video, he is given 10 minutes and the final output boasts near-perfect ratios, shadow and a background — quite amazing. Next, the artist has 60 seconds and the result is an image that is unmistakably Spiderman with neck and torso, but rough. Finally, he has just 10 seconds and can only rush out the sketch of a misshapen head and crude eyes, though it is still, just, recognizable as the comic-book superhero. The task 'draw Spiderman' was completed and was usefully sharable (with a 9-year-old niece, say) and therefore good enough in all three cases. A pixel-perfect rendition of Spiderman's left eye or chin would not have passed the usefully sharable test and would therefore likely not be deemed good enough by the hypothetical niece.

Over 250 years ago, Voltaire suggested that, 'The perfect is the enemy of the good,'[58] meaning that in striving for perfection we can miss out on achieving good or even excellent outcomes. It's still true now. Usefully shareable, on the other hand, is a staunch supporter of the good.

Outside world

Your labour is more valuable if someone is able to taste its fruits. Usefully shareable is a handy heuristic for deciding when you've reached a 'good enough' standard. Several additional benefits emerge as your work encounters the outside world:

- **Different perspectives.** By sharing with others, you can get additional input on the work from people with different viewpoints and experiences. For many tasks, such a diversity of perspectives and collective intelligence is highly valuable, for some it's essential.
- **Iteration.** Sharing elicits feedback, which enables iterative improvement.
- **Buy-in.** If you share at the right time and with the right intention, you can bring collaborators along on the journey with you. This contrasts with presenting them at the end with a fait accompli, which can irritate, strike discord and generate needless resistance.
- **Credit.** If someone sees what you've done, you may receive appreciation or praise, or just enhance your reputation and status generally. If no one at all sees it, no such credit will be forthcoming.
- **Collective productivity.** Your part has been played, for now. Pass the baton on, so that your work can continue its journey while your attention is needed elsewhere. Big or small, we are all cogs in a machine. And if we consider that machine to be a collective human endeavour, the parts we play may seem worthwhile.
  The principle applies as much to sharing a paradigm-changing idea to inspire humankind as it does to hanging out the washing to clothe the family.

Of course, a lot of the time we'll need to share our work anyway: a boss demands it, a colleague expects it, a friend relies on it. But by keeping in mind the wide-ranging benefits listed above, we are encouraged to share something even more than we strictly need to.

■ ■ ■ ■

To deliver our work, to present the fruits of our labour — to ship something — is satisfying. There's an intrinsic reward for its completion as well as an extrinsic reward for sending it on. Viewed this way and practised properly, we might come to enjoy as many as fifteen rewards, in the form of duly completed timeboxes, every single day.

Shipping also increases productivity. As we saw in *Chapter 6 — To collaborate*, timeboxing is about collective as well as individual productivity. Unshared work is like a bird in a gilded cage. So, do something good enough, and get it out there.

Review

- Perfection is neither necessary nor possible, so get comfortable and familiar with good enough.
- The standard you've achieved is 'good enough' when what you've done is usefully shareable.
- We can use the concept of Minimum Viable Product to help determine what is usefully shareable.
- Sharing or shipping your work has many benefits, including:
  - gaining different perspectives
  - the chance to iterate
  - getting buy-in from others

- earning credit from others
- keeping the project moving, even as your attention is elsewhere.

Reflect

- Think of a piece of work you were proud of and shared to good effect. Use that example as your gold standard for shipping something.
- Watch the Spiderman video referenced in this chapter.
- Do you feel you have a good enough sense of what good enough or usefully shareable is? If not, how could you refine it further in the context of your own work and life?

Oh dear! Oh dear! I shall be too late!

— The White Rabbit (from *Alice in Wonderland*)

18. Rabbit holes & other distractions

Keywords	Distraction; preconditions; environment; prompts; response; rabbit holes; multitasking; single-tasking; sidetrack; focus; procrastination
Word count	3,559
Read time	18 mins

This is the chapter I most looked forward to writing.

You've come a long way already on your timeboxing journey. You're aware of the benefits and therefore, I hope, have resolved to establish and maintain this method and mindset. You've chosen some worthwhile tasks and planned them sensibly, and your resolve has strengthened. You've come to understand what good practice looks and feels like as you're in the timebox, carrying out the task itself.

Yet difficult moments lie ahead. For the duration of each and every one of your many forthcoming timeboxes, there are a thousand distractions lurking. Your phone vibrates. An alarm sounds. A browser notification notifies. A hyperlink beckons. The distraction might be prompted internally: a thought occurs, a memory surfaces, an itch irks. These are all common, generic distractions that affect us all. We all have our own idiosyncratic prompts of distraction.

There is no bullet-proof barricade against distractions but there are some sensible protective measures we can take, starting by understanding what distractions are and where they come from. My role is to bring up generic situations with enough flesh and flavour to resonate with you. Your role is to use the examples to think about which of these (or other) distractions crop up and do damage in your life. You will then be well placed to implement your own nuanced solutions.

A fundamental and useful framework for thinking about distractions is in terms of the **preconditions** in which procrastination thrives, the **prompts** that divert our attention and our **responses** to those prompts. If we can understand how these work and inter-relate, we will do a better job of optimizing those preconditions, reducing the prompts and improving our responses to them.

Optimize the preconditions — nip procrastination in the bud

Sometimes there's a problem before we've even begun and it goes by the name of procrastination: putting off something we know we should do. Procrastination is widespread: 20% of adults[59] are chronic procrastinators and the proportion is much higher among students.[60] Timeboxing hits procrastination pretty hard and from multiple angles: starting small, structure, accountability and, as Dr Timothy Pychyl, author of *Solving the Procrastination Puzzle*, puts it, the 'real mood boost [that] comes from doing what we intend to do'. And yet, at times, this strange, insidious reluctance will persist.

There are many underlying causes of, and contributing factors to, procrastination. Some of these overlap and interrelate and most are not fully understood. I've listed some of the most common causes here in the expectation that several will resonate with you, and the hope that you will give extra attention to those that resonate most. The items at the top are harder to resolve, the items at the bottom, easier:

- anxiety, stress and other mental health issues
- not having the right mindset or sufficient motivation
- fear of failure or perfectionism
- a reluctance to tackle a difficult task

- boredom
- tiredness, fatigue or burnout
- a lack of structure, specificity or deadlines
- overwhelm when faced with too many tasks or too large a task; you don't know where to begin.

This is not an exhaustive list. And it falls beyond the scope of this book to propose or expound on specific solutions to the more complex issues towards the top. The practice of timeboxing helps most people to some extent with all of the impediments listed above. But even timeboxing is not a panacea for deep-rooted or long-standing psychological issues; if some of these are factors for you, you may need to address them with due seriousness by seeking appropriate help from professionals in these areas.

Since some of this is difficult, be sure to do the easy things. Lessen the effect of many of these underlying causes by working on mindset and environment. All the advice about achieving the right mindset and the right environment (in Chapter 9) when planning your timebox (for 15 minutes a day) applies as much, if not more, when carrying out the timeboxes themselves (many hours a day). Don't attempt difficult tasks when you are tired, fatigued or burnt out. The last two items in the list are thoroughly thwarted by timeboxing, which provides explicit structure, specificity and deadlines and avowedly filters out all but one thing to address overwhelm head-to-head, one-to-one.

Personally, I've noticed that I'm most vulnerable to the fourth (too difficult) and fifth (too dull) items on the list above. If the task is challenging in certain ways (physically demanding exercise, an adversarial work situation, an intellectually difficult problem), I find ways to avoid it. And if it's too easy or lacks any kind of intrigue or surprise or weight, I also turn elsewhere. Note that these troublesome conditions are exactly the conditions that inhibit us from achieving a just-right challenge and entering into Csíkszentmihályi's state of flow (see *Chapter 5 — To think smarter*).

Notice and minimize prompts

You've started, you're in the timebox, but an event intrudes and whisks you out of it, suddenly. What are these moments of mischief? I find it helpful to think about distracting prompts in terms of the *medium* in which they manifest (mental, digital and physical), along with their level of *urgency*. The medium helps us think about what they are and where they come from; the level of urgency helps us take the appropriate action. This way of thinking gives rise to a table:

	Digital	Physical	Mental
Non-urgent	• a notification • an email • a text • you sit back down at your computer after a break and look around the screen for what's most interesting	• a bird flies by • a mosquito vexes you • your dog starts barking • you hear your kids are watching TV when they shouldn't be	• you idly wonder whether roosters actually make the sound COCK-A-DOODLE-DO • you recollect a fragment of last night's dream • you wonder if you have any new emails/messages • you become thirsty • you start to feel bored • you remember a big work task that you'll need to complete next week

Urgent	• An email comes through calling for immediate action	• someone knocks at the front door • your baby cries • an unplanned fire alarm sounds • someone shouts your name • you need to go to the bathroom	• you have what feels like an important idea — an epiphany • you remember you left your keys behind in the shop you were just in • you remember the dentist appointment you have that day (but didn't calendarize)

Note that non-urgent items may very well be *important*, e.g. the big work task example above. The key distinction in terms of taking *immediate* action is whether there's *urgency*, not whether there's importance.

And these prompts are just that, the start — it sets off a powerful mechanism. There's no telling at the outset quite how deep the rabbit hole goes. You might hit a dead end and emerge in a minute or two. Or one fascinating turn may take another and, all of a sudden, a couple of hours have disappeared.

The table is intended to help you notice distractions when they happen. You will notice them more easily if you look for them and expect to see them in any of the three domains — digital, physical and mental. Such distractions are common for everyone. The examples here are intended to be real and resonate with readers, but if you can think of an example for each of the six boxes, this chapter will serve you all the better. Most importantly, the table provides a framework for preparing different, better *responses* to the different kinds of prompts. By understanding that noticing is valuable, with a little practice, we slowly, surely hone the skill.

Some prompts occur many times in our lives. A few of them occur multiple times a day: most of us pick up our phones over a hundred times a day. These are, of course, the most devastating types of prompts, as they attack our intentional productivity so often. It's worth spending a couple of minutes now thinking about which these might be for you. Is it when you return to your desk? Is it when your phone vibrates? Is it seeing the number of notifications in your inbox go up by one at the top of a browser tab? Is it when you get home and see housework in every direction? These recurrent distractions are opportunities for you to make the biggest improvements to your life.

Improve your response

We human beings have the chance to choose what we do. As Viktor Frankl brilliantly puts it, 'Between stimulus and response there is a space. In that space is our power to choose our response. In our response lies our growth and our freedom.'

But in general, modern humans' responses to prompts are shambolic. We tend not to notice the prompt, we aren't aware of the space Frankl refers to and so, of course, we don't use it. Instead, we react without thinking and without intention — as if we have no cognitive ability to interject wilfully. Working through some of the examples in the table above, we:

- Reply to that Slack notification or email.*
- Click on several of our open browser tabs, and end up shopping, searching or surfing.
- Go downstairs to check on the dogs, see there's some washing that needs taking out, and discover that there's another load that should really go in.

- See one bird flying by and then notice two others, and alongside them a passing cloud . . . that resembles an armchair and we're daydreaming.
- Google 'cock-a-doodle-do', which takes us to a nursery rhyme, which sparks a curiosity about fiddling sticks, which . . .
- Open a second document and get started on a second piece of work, without having finished the first.*

We attempt to multitask (asterisked items) or we disappear down rabbit holes. At their worst, multitasking and rabbit holes are very bad news: they destroy productivity and reduce our feeling of accomplishment. Worse still, in some cases, we're indulging and feeding harmful addictions (to social media, obsessive work, messaging platforms, etc.). They negate the peace, productivity and power of timeboxing. On the other hand, at their best, multitasking and rabbit holes can be a joy, and we'll cover that too, shortly.

So, how should we respond instead?

As we've seen, first we need to notice the prompt. This act of noticing is a prerequisite for everything else here, the space for us to choose our response. This is a skill that we can develop through awareness and practice.

After that, we need to decide, quickly, whether the distraction requires urgent action. Do you really need to attend to it right now? Occasionally, the answer will truly be 'yes' (such as with most of the examples in the bottom row of boxes in the table). In these rare cases, of course, do what you need to do, make that immediate change of plan — and don't forget to update the timeboxes in your calendar when you can. Far, far more often though, the answer will be 'no'. Then, if it's something you will want to come back to later, jot it down (avoid the excruciating feeling of a fading, fleeting thought by pinning it down on your to-do list or, if you don't have access in the moment, utter it out loud — verbalize it) and come back to your scheduled timebox. Or, if the distraction is something you can dismiss right away, do so and come straight back to the timebox (return to calendar). As a diagram, this is how it flows:

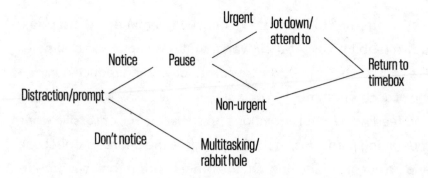

There are tactics that can help here. Encourage the better, more intentional response of returning to your timebox by making some appropriate adjustments to your environment (see *Chapter 9 — The basics*).

You will soon come to associate the prompt with the response of returning to the safe haven of your timebox.

Rabbit holes

We all go down rabbit holes sometimes. The human mind and the hyperlinked internet are fertile grounds for compelling curiosities, and they feed off each other.

Rabbit holes can be joyous. They can be a delightful, exquisite feature of human experience — useful and exhilarating. But this abandon and loss of control, which can feel so good, might turn bad. Does the following sound familiar?

You start the task as planned. But an unexpected link, phrase or image piques your interest. 'What's this?' you wonder, curious. Before your awareness has time to act, you've clicked the link and chased the rabbit. You're undergoing a whole new experience now, which has your entire, intense focus. Another item catches your eye and you're further still from the intended task. Utterly engrossed, you've lost sense of time, enter a state of flow and take one turn after another — curiouser and curiouser.[61] Eventually, the adventure's excitement subsides and a moment of realization hits: you've strayed a long way from where you began. You come back out of the rabbit hole and return to the task at hand but you've lost time, maybe lots of it.

When it happens — and it will happen often, with or without timeboxing — don't berate yourself. Any guilt or worry you might feel is unnecessary, unwarranted, unhelpful and . . . itself a further distraction. The trick is to avoid them in the first place (optimize the preconditions), notice the prompts and respond by coming back to the timebox. You'll begin to link the feeling of stress, over-whelm or panic with the reassuring thought and act of returning to the calendar (by clicking on your top-left browser tab).

Multitasking

Most of us multitask. On the face of it, multitasking is antithetical to timeboxing, a method that espouses the power of doing one thing at a time. But is it?

First, what is it? Multitasking is the attempt to do several things at once. It involves splitting our attention across multiple tasks, usually with the goal of getting more done in less time. The concept came from computing where, many decades ago, computers could only do one thing at a time.

Multitasking is a much maligned and misunderstood practice. Some research and a slew of recent online content on this topic take a dim view of it. Context switching, it's argued, is cognitively expensive, and most takes conclude that multitasking is down-right bad for productivity. There's a seminal video[62] demonstrating inattentional blindness in which a group of people are passing a basketball between them. Viewers are asked to count the number of passes made by players wearing white. At least half the viewers fail to spot the gorilla that makes its way across the playing area for several seconds halfway through the video. We are not able to pay attention to two things at once, then. Science has spoken, case closed.

Indeed, there are situations in which multitasking unarguably fails: half-heartedly perusing social media while talking to a friend or partner; texting while driving; coding while chatting; worrying about two things at once; looking after kids while analysing data. One of the most common and damaging examples is when we open a hard-hitting email (the type that sends us into a spin of thoughts and feelings) during a meeting, making ourselves unable to contribute effectively to either (notice how much better off we are if we can simply muster the discipline to hold off on the email until after the meeting). We all have our own personal examples of attempts at multitasking that ended in abject failure.

And yet sometimes it seems to be just fine: cooking a meal while listening to a podcast; jogging while mulling over a difficult problem; casually shopping from your phone while winding down in front of the television; painting ceramics while getting to know someone on a first date.

In fact, multitasking can work. According to one study,[63] 'The secret to multitasking to make better use of your time ultimately lies in finding tasks that don't cause a huge amount of conflict with each other', and, in particular, that it can only really work with certain *well-practised* tasks where the cognitive demand and conflict are low. Of course, well-practised means different things to different people.

Overleaf is a table with a small sample of work and non-work-related tasks, indicating which can be carried out in tandem, and which can't. But, of course and as always, what's important is how these kinds of pairs work (or otherwise) for *you*.

How to read this chart

1. Choose two activities for which you'd like to check compatibility. To illustrate, let's pick 'Cooking' and 'Attending a meeting'.
2. Find the column labelled 'Cooking' (your first chosen activity).
3. Now, find the row labelled 'Attending a meeting' (your second chosen activity).
4. Navigate down the 'Cooking' column until you reach the row for 'Attending a meeting.'

5. The symbol displayed where the column and row intersect indicates the activities' compatibility. ✔ means compatibility; ✘ means incompatible; ? suggests that the activities might work together under certain circumstances.

6. In our example, 'Cooking' and 'Attending a meeting' intersect at the ? symbol. This suggests that though they aren't possible simultaneously in all situations, you could, for example, attend a meeting off-camera with headphones while cooking.

Mowing

Mowing	Cooking	Reading	Emailing	Attending a mtg	Laundry	Diffusive thinking	Gentle exercise	
✘	Cooking							
✘	✘	Reading						
✘	✘	✘	Emailing					
✘	?	✘	?	Attending a mtg				
✘	✘	✘	✘	✘	Laundry			
✔	✔	✘	✘	✘	✔	Diffusive thinking		
✘	✘	?	✔	✔	?	✔	Gentle exercise	
✘	✘	✘	✘	✘	✘	?	✘	Hard exercise

For some of these to work, we may need to use a little imagination. For example, gentle exercise is just about possible when attending a meeting, but the exercise will need to be very carefully chosen (finger strength exercises, bouncing on a Pilates ball, a walking treadmill in a home office). Reading a book is tricky while cooking but listening to an audiobook can work.

Other pairs here will depend on the context — specifically the strengths and characteristics of the individual as well as the level of performance required. For example, one of the most common and notorious pairings is email and meetings; should someone be emailing and thereby not fully attending to what their colleagues are saying? It's not clear. What if the meeting is only tangentially relevant to the offending emailer? Or if there's an urgent email that needs sending during a long meeting? The context matters, so think about it, decide what works best for you and make your preferred ways of working and living clear to those you work and live with.

There are countless pairs that I have not included in this sample table, including difficult items like worrying/ruminating, which can be, simultaneously, about two distinct concerns. This is an issue for many of us.

Indeed, there are even situations where performance may be *enhanced* by a second activity. When our diffuse thinking mode unlocks what our focused thinking mode has failed to. Or when a single activity is too easy, we may become bored and discard it unless it's accompanied by a second activity (e.g. folding clothes and listening to a podcast). There may even be cognitive advantages to multitasking; in one study,[64] participants who multitasked with media most frequently became more effective at multisensory integration (the brain's ability to combine and process information from the five senses — vision, hearing, touch, taste and smell).

In the notable situations when multitasking works, timeboxing is just as appropriate and useful. Choose the symbiotic pair of activities carefully and intentionally, describe the timebox accordingly and then multitask within the single timebox happily and productively. The purpose of timeboxing and of this book is to help us use our time well, not to be dogmatic. And for the many more situations in which multitasking doesn't work (though you find yourself so indulging): notice, pause, jot down if you need to, and return placidly and without reproach to your timebox.

■ ■ ■ ■

Distractions are inevitable. Accepting them is part of life and part of timeboxing. By understanding the preconditions, prompts and responses to them, you will be much better placed to keep closer to your intentions and exert greater influence on your life. You won't be able to and don't need to do any of this perfectly. You just need to use it to move in the right direction to reap rewards.

Review

- Distractions threaten timeboxing.
- The distraction can be broken down into: the pre-conditions that make them favourable, the prompting events that get them started, and our responses to them.
- By developing an awareness of them, we can improve the situation on all three fronts.
- Rabbit holes can hurt productivity (as well as bring joy).
- Multitasking can also hurt productivity (as well as bring joy).
- Certain pairs of activities can be carried out simultaneously; others cannot. Find out which pairs work for you.

Reflect

- What are the ways in which you most often get sidetracked from your intended goal?
- You will get distracted away from your timeboxes, away from this book, several times, even today. Try to notice when this happens and how you respond. Think about how you might prevent the prompt. Think about how you might improve your response.
- Make a physical, visual aid to help draw you back out of rabbit holes — a small sign or sticker that says 'Return to Calendar' or a mousepad with an image that will serve the same purpose or, even better, a message that you've thought up yourself. Place it somewhere you'll see it when you need to, e.g. by your workstation or on your phone case.
- Construct your own table of activities that can or cannot be carried out simultaneously. Which pairs seem to work for you? Which pairs could be made to work with a little imagination?

PART FOUR — OWN

∎ ∎ ∎ ∎

The final part is about keeping timeboxing with you and making it your own. The promise of an intentional life can only be realized with concerted effort over years and decades and through the three major segments of our lives: work, leisure and sleep.

One Ring to rule them all,
One Ring to find them,
One Ring to bring them all
and in the darkness bind them.

— J.R.R. Tolkien

19. Build the habit

Keywords	Routine; behaviour; prompt; motivation; reward; anchoring; habit-stacking
Word count	2,222
Read time	11 mins

For timeboxing to bear fruit over the course of your life, you'll need to do it consistently. And you're much more likely to do it consistently if it becomes a habit. If it doesn't, what was learnt from this book will eventually dissipate. But if it does, you open the door to becoming the person you want to be, do the things you want to do, and choose a life you will come to cherish.

We all have good and bad habits. Many of us routinely exercise, eat healthily, meditate, practise good hygiene, work hard, look in on neighbours, read, learn, and more. Yet we're also a species that bites its nails, gambles compulsively, scrolls absent-mindedly, shops needlessly, binges on media, indulges in junk food, procrastinates, and worse.

Timeboxing is a meta-habit that can build and govern other habits. The good habits just listed could all themselves be timeboxed. Timeboxing is the single, primary habit which can help us develop multiple secondary habits. I like to think of timeboxing as the one habit to rule them all.

How habits work

A wealth of science and popular literature on the subject of habits has sprung up over the past decade or so. Nir Eyal's *Hooked* showed us how Big Tech designs products to get us just that.

James Clear's *Atomic Habits* introduced millions to the idea of making habits stick by making behaviour easier. Both of these and many other authors have drawn on the decades-long work of BJ Fogg on behaviour change and habit formation. Scientists, neurobiologists, behaviourists, anthropologists and many other kinds of experts have added to a growing understanding of the subject in an era of screen time and digital dopamine.

I've chosen the Fogg Behavior Model to explain why building timeboxing into a habit is supremely straightforward. It's the simplest and, to my mind, most natural. He breaks behaviour down like this:

Behaviour = Motivation × Ability × Prompt

The model states that a behavior (including a habit) will happen when motivation, ability, and a prompt come together at the same moment.

For example, a behaviour might be to re-read this chapter. You might do that because:

- You're motivated (you recognize that turning timeboxing into a habit is important and you haven't quite grasped how to do that on your first reading).
- You're able to (re-reading a single chapter is not difficult).
- You're prompted to by reading this set of bullet points.

Recall that there are two components to timeboxing: planning (Part Two) and doing (Part Three). They are interdependent: we're more likely to keep planning the timeboxes if we end up getting them done; and we're more likely to get them done if we've planned them. We need both for timeboxing to become a solid habit.

You'll soon see that you are already motivated, able and prompted to timebox. As such, building a reliable habit of time-boxing each day will be easier than you might think.

Motivation

At this point you've read more than 200 pages of a book about timeboxing. It's safe to assume that you already have some motivation to timebox.

But if you feel you need a top-up, remind yourself of the benefits laid out in Part One. There are six: for the record, for serenity, to think smarter, to collaborate, for productivity, and for an intentional life. Even better, pick the one benefit that means most to you, turn that into a readily recalled mantra, and remind yourself of it as part of your prompt (written on the Post-it note, the screen-saver, the scheduled email, etc.)

Another way to boost motivation is to associate the planning of your day with an activity you relish. For example, if you enjoy a morning coffee, plan your day during the 15 minutes it takes to drink it. A positive association like this will help to make timeboxing an activity you feel good about.

What about rewards to increase motivation? There are several emotional rewards that you can associate with planning time-boxes. First, you can embrace the positive feeling that you've started your day in the right way; it can be satisfying to see a fully timeboxed day laid out neatly before you. Second, timeboxing can help you feel less anxious about the day ahead. Tap into this sense of relief, which in itself is a reward that will make your habit stronger. If you share your calendar with others, you may even feel an element of social satisfaction. As Fogg points out, emotional rewards like these help us to form and strengthen a habit.

Completing a timebox should bring a sense of accomplishment. Each of these is a bona fide success and should feel good. Don't resist that good feeling — embrace it! Perhaps you mark the occasion by ticking it off physically on paper, digitally with an emoji or just in your head as an acknowledgement. At the end of the day or the week, take a look back at what you did. It will be a lot.

Make timeboxing fun. *Chapter 16 — Pacing & racing* is largely about this. A dull, easy or boring task (entering data into a spreadsheet, expunging an inbox, doing the dishes) may become an interesting challenge if you apply a time constraint.

At times, you may need to be tough with yourself. Set aside excuses and remind yourself of who you want to be — an intentional person, leading the life you choose. You might find it useful to visualize, exaggerate even, the downside of *not* timeboxing: the feeling of disappointment, being frazzled, the implications of not getting things done — even guilt and shame can be used advantageously here. As the neurobiologist Andrew Huberman puts it, 'foreshadowing failure is more effective than picturing success'.

Finally, remember that *you* are the ultimate source of motivation. It was a higher power that decided on the particular sequence of scheduled activities you see before you on your calendar. That higher power was you, you in a better moment, during the calm before the day's storm. Who better to listen to than that? Your earlier self can be the motivating guardian of your present self, if your present self will only listen.

Ability

A key concept in the Fogg Behavior Model is this: the easier a behaviour is to do, the less motivation we need for it. Likewise, the harder the behaviour, the higher the levels of motivation required. So, even though you have plenty of motivation already, let's make timeboxing as *easy* as possible.

For planning the timeboxes, the requirement is just 15 minutes' effort to improve the rest of your day. It's a bargain! Still, make the first step as small as you can. Rather than 15 minutes of planning your day, have in mind what your very first action will be. Fogg calls this the 'starter step'. When you timebox, your starter step might be to open up a Microsoft Outlook or Google Calendar. Or it might be to close your eyes for 60 seconds and observe which priorities manifest. Identify the very first element of how you will actually plan your timebox in the smallest possible terms. Make sure that it's easy, tangible and practical. Once you've taken your starter step, the rest of the planning of your day is far more likely to follow.

For carrying out (doing) the timeboxes, the requirement is a mere single task. Just one. Sometimes it won't be glamorous or fun or easy. But it's just one thing, hand-picked by you a short while ago, to liberate you from a thousand others. Besides, you don't need to do it for long — just 15 (or 30 or 60) minutes.

Prompt

A prompt is anything that says, 'Do this behaviour now'. Some prompts happen in our natural environment, like raindrops prompting us to open an umbrella. But for many other habits, such as timeboxing, we need to design the prompt.

What will be the prompt that reminds you to plan your time-boxes every day? For those of us who use a digital calendar, the answer is easy: it's the 15-minute calendar entry at the start of our day. In Chapter 9 I urged (prompted!) you to add this recurring timebox to your calendar. If you didn't do it then, please do it now (your second prompt).

Give this daily calendar appointment every chance to succeed as a prompt. To work for you, you'll need to see it in time, every single day. If you already habitually look at your calendar first thing, you won't miss it and you won't have a problem. But if you start your day with some other activity, work out how to get from that morning activity to the 'Timebox today' appointment in your calendar.

Here are some examples:

- If you go to the bathroom to brush your teeth or take a shower in the morning, put a sign up on the mirror or by the door that reminds you to open your calendar.
- If your first activity is to make yourself a cup of coffee, stick a Post-it note on the kitchen cupboard where you keep coffee mugs.
- If you read news online on your tablet first thing, create a (daily) reminder on your device to go to your calendar next.

Whichever behaviour or routine you choose to get yourself to start timeboxing, think in particular about its *very last act*. Fogg calls this the 'trailing edge' of the behaviour. Suppose your first activity is to take a shower. What's the *very last part* of that process? Is it to put clothes in the laundry basket, turn the bathroom light off, spray on some aftershave or perfume, or something else? Whatever it is, use *that* as your prompt to go and timebox. This is a little harder if you're not in the same physical space or room as where you'd like to timebox your day. In this case, it might be effective to keep the prompt in mind through this transition by literally saying something like 'Next up, I'm timeboxing my day' out loud a few times, until you finally get to the place where you're going to timebox.

This method of pinning the behaviour you're trying to develop (timeboxing) to an existing, established habit (shower, coffee, tablet) is called 'anchoring' by Fogg. James Clear later used the term 'habit stacking'.[65]

And what are the prompts to get you to do your timeboxes through the day? Also easy: it's the series of timeboxes you've made in your calendar. You just need to stay close to your calendar.

Of course, as you go through your day things will sometimes happen that may take you away from timeboxing. Your phone rings, your daughter asks you a question, someone knocks on the door. The key here is to recognize that you've gone off track. And this moment of recognition is your prompt to return to your calendar, to your timeboxes. For example, many of us sit down to our computer multiple times a day (after breaks, meetings, etc). Our positive prompt is the timeboxed calendar itself, but that will only be effective if we encounter it. So, when you sit down to resume work, what happens, exactly? Do you lift up your laptop screen? If so, place a sticker on the lid to remind you to return to calendar. Or is the first thing you see your screensaver? Then make that screensaver a return-to-calendar message. Do you pull out a stool? Again, a relevant, well-placed sticker might serve to remind, just when you need it.

■ ■ ■ ■

Timeboxing is not a brand-new behaviour. We all already have appointments, meetings and schedules and most of us already use a digital calendar. So, the habit you need to form is the extension of an existing behaviour, not the establishment of a brand-new one. Your odds are good. In fact, it's quite possible that you'll be able to build timeboxing into a habit in the time you take to read this book.

The habits that matter are the habits that stick. Take the advice here and you'll soon be timeboxing with sublime, unconscious competence, and establishing secondary habits with ease.

Review

- Timeboxing consistently will make a big difference to your whole life.
- Timeboxing serves as a foundational habit that can guide and organize multiple other habits.
- The Fogg Behavior Model says: Behaviour = Motivation x Ability x Prompt. All three components are required for a habit to form. You already have all three to a large extent.
- Anchor timeboxing (planning and doing) to an existing habit to make it easier still.
- Timeboxing is not new. It's an extension and enhancement of existing behaviour (any use of your calendar) and this will make it much easier to adopt as a habit.

Reflect

- Check in on both your motivation and ability to timebox. How could you increase either?
- Send an email to your future self (an email scheduled to send in one month's time) about the reasons you've decided to start timeboxing. When you get the email, ask yourself if timeboxing has now become a habit for you.
- Notice when you struggle to start or complete a timebox. Is it when a task is boring? Or hard? Or when the task is for certain people? Or when the appointment is automated?
- Download a return-to-calendar screensaver from marczaosanders.com/rtc. Or, even better, make one yourself.

No time like the present.

— Mary Manley

20. As mindfulness

Keywords	Mind control; meditation; Zen; the present moment; sanctuary; agency; analogy
Word count	917
Read time	5 mins

It may be helpful and inspiring to think of timeboxing as a highly pragmatic and accessible form of mindfulness. Helpful, if you have some experience of being mindful and the practices that help achieve a mindful state. And inspiring if you hold aspirations to lead a more mindful life. Mindfulness is:

The mental state of being fully present, aware of where we are and what we're doing, and not overly reactive to or distracted by what's going on around us.

It may occur to you, as you read this definition, that timeboxing shares several of these characteristics. Yet timeboxing is easier and more accessible, for some of us.

Mindfulness and timeboxing are alike

The similarities are many and striking. I describe just a few here.

Both are about developing greater control over our minds. We embark on a goal that requires some mental exertion, we encounter distractions, we become aware of the distraction — a metacognitive skill — and bring ourselves back, without judgement or blame, to our intended activity. A short, mindful pause (which might itself be timeboxed) between two meetings creates a cognitive buffer to separate the mental activity of the first from the second, improving the experience of both and demonstrating how the two methods can combine. Both help us to develop our agency as well as our feeling of agency.

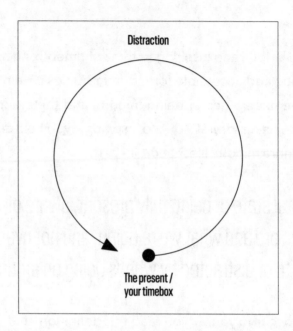

Both also protect us from feeling overwhelmed. Mindfulness helps us to deal with the stupefying volume of sensory data and information we are exposed to each day and focus on and savour what matters. Timeboxing helps us to cope with the staggering number of choices we face at any given moment; pick one, drop the rest, and attend only to the single, singular thing that matters. Both are methods of focusing attention from the impossibly many to just one thing. Both provide protection against thoughts and feelings that might unsettle us: a refuge and shelter, a safe space and stronghold; even a sanctuary, haven, oasis.

Both give us access to the higher power that is ourself in an earlier, tranquil, better moment. Mindfulness helps us to access, notice and understand our innermost thoughts and deeply held emotions — the aspects of our life that are truly exciting or frightening or important to us at the time. Timeboxing provides a constant link back to the crisp thinking and planning of our undistracted, unruffled selves.

Both prioritize the present over the past or the future. Mindfulness directs our attention to the present moment. As Sam Harris puts it: 'The future never arrives.'[66] Similarly, with timeboxing, there's a sense in which there's only really ever the timebox you're in. Timeboxing consistently encourages us to engage with the box-shaped present.

Both can cultivate gratitude. Mindfulness encourages a sense of gratitude and appreciation for the present moment and the blessings in our lives that might otherwise be taken for granted. Timeboxing reminds us that the vast, overwhelming, burdensome choice we face is a privilege that few other humans in the history of the species have had the chance to enjoy.

The ultimate benefits of timeboxing (described in Part One) coincide with those of mindfulness. Mindfulness enables us to know ourselves better through self-awareness. To achieve a level of serenity through acceptance. To think smarter through clarity. To collaborate better through empathy and kindness. To get more done through focus. And to lead a good life through intention.

But timeboxing is easier

For at least two and a half millennia, people have derived enormous benefits from the practice of mindfulness, to gain insights, reduce stress and enhance well-being.

But effecting and maintaining this kind of conscious state, moment to moment, is not easy. It's ethereal and ephemeral. It's hard to know when you've achieved mindfulness. And impossible for anyone else to know if you have. Timeboxing, on the other hand, is more like a good book you hold in your hands, utterly accessible, stable and solid.

A timebox is tangible. It's an appointment in your calendar. You can point to it. You can edit it. It tells you precisely what to do and when. It's not one little bit elusive.

A timebox is forgiving. In a 30-minute window, say, you have the time to go wrong, become distracted, notice the distraction and get back on track, multiple times if necessary.

A timebox's success or failure is clear. We complete the task within the time, or we don't. We pass or we fail. Either way, we reflect and improve. But that feedback loop is firmer and more instructive for having an explicit outcome.

None of this chapter nor any of this book is intended to undermine the tradition of mindfulness. But perhaps for some people, timeboxing, being easier and more tangible, may serve as a stepping stone towards mindful living.

■ ■ ■ ■

Timeboxing and mindfulness can help each other. Thinking of the two together can make timeboxing more appealing and mindfulness more attainable.

Review

- Mindfulness and timeboxing share many characteristics.
- Timeboxing is more accessible, for many.
- Timeboxing can be used as a path towards mindfulness.

Reflect

- What other similarities do you see between mindfulness and timeboxing?
- In which other situations do you actively refocus your attention? When are you best at this? When are you worst?
- Set a 15-minute timebox to meditate on timeboxing. Close your eyes, call timeboxing to mind and observe what occurs to you in that time. Afterwards, write down what you remember. Now, are there any additional similarities you see between the practices of mindfulness and timeboxing?

Rest and be thankful.

— William Wordsworth

21. Better breaks

Keywords	Rest; recovery; energy; rejuvenation; pause; time-off; relax; chill; close your eyes; breathe; deep breath
Word count	1,414
Read time	8 mins

We don't think enough about how best to take breaks. Most of us take them when we're mentally or physically exhausted and not in the ideal state to choose how best to spend the time. Instead, as with the timeboxing of tasks, let's find a way to be more intentional about breaks, rest and rejuvenation.

Breaks are essential. A study conducted by Microsoft in 2021[67] used electroencephalograms (EEGs) to compare beta wave activity (associated with stress) between participants in back-to-back virtual meetings and those taking short (10-minute) breaks in between. The experiment yielded three insights. First, breaks enable our brains to reset, reducing the cumulative build-up of stress that a hectic day can bring. Second, they produced positive levels of frontal alpha asymmetry (associated with, among other benefits, an increased ability to focus and be engaged). Third, the transition from one meeting straight to the next caused a spike in stress. Breaks help us to feel and perform better.

Breaks are important but we all need and get different things from them. We'll mostly focus on intraday breaks here, but we'll also take a brief stop at weekends and holidays.

In many jurisdictions, there are even legal responsibilities for employers and rights for employees. For example, in the UK, anyone working more than 4½ hours in a single stretch is entitled to a rest break of at least 30 minutes.

I assume that most people reading this book are aware of and in receipt of their legal rights. I'll also assume — as I have throughout the book — that you have some room to choose and plan your breaks.

So then, why, what and for how long?

For what purpose?

I'll categorize break-related activities by their *purpose*. This speaks to the intentionality of timeboxing and the agency that the method draws on and brings out. So, while it's valid to divide them up in other ways (e.g. social, diversion, learning and so on), that wouldn't get to the crux of it, the *why*. We take breaks:

- **For our minds.** To rest or divert the brain in order to reduce stress and bring it to prime condition for whatever's next.
- **For our bodies.** To nourish our flesh and bones. Note that this might be achieved in many ways, from inactivity to intense activity.
- **To reward our achievements.** As we saw in Chapter 19, rewards help motivate and incentivize, establish positive connections in our brains between the response and the reward and consolidate sound practice into established habit.

The activities we may choose to engage in (see below) fall into one or more of these categories and we should choose them for the purpose(s) they serve.

Breaks are also used by many for productive, non-core purposes, such as admin or learning or to further our careers. Though these are, of course, commendable pursuits, in my view they are *tasks* and, as such, should be given the standard timeboxing treatment.

What to do in them

There are so many possibilities! Yet most of us don't actively consider the wide menu of options at our disposal. Let's put that right with a selection of some of the most common restful practices, each classified with one of the three purposes described above:

Activity	For mind	For body	To reward
Meditate	✔		✔
Take a power nap	✔	✔	✔
Just close your eyes momentarily	✔		
Undertake a breathing exercise	✔	✔	✔
Get off screens	✔	✔	
Take a short walk[68]	✔	✔	✔
Eat a snack		✔	✔
Drink a drink	✔	✔	✔
Gaze outside (at nature if possible)	✔	✔	✔
Do a high-intensity workout, like a fast-paced run		✔	
Do a low-intensity workout, like yin yoga	✔	✔	✔
Talk to a colleague	✔		✔
Reconnect with someone	✔		✔
Check your messages			✔
Read a book	✔		✔
Tidy your desk space	✔		✔

Psych yourself up for a high-stakes next meeting[69]	✔		
Get into nature	✔	✔	✔
Daydream	✔		
Stretch	✔	✔	✔
Call a family member	✔		✔
Read an article you've been looking forward to	✔		✔
Show someone some gratitude	✔		✔
Journal	✔		
Doodle	✔		✔
Pray	✔		✔
Take a toilet break		✔	

Any of the above can, and should, be adapted for your context. For example, the right kind of food or drink to ingest will vary from person to person, but take a look at the science — there's a difference, for example, between the effect of protein-, carbohydrate- and fat-containing drinks on cognitive performance.[70] Some books can serve you with rest and reward; some do quite the opposite. Ditto colleagues and family members. So, for different situations, pick the most suitable break activity from the many, many options at your disposal.

The list above is intended to be inclusive and non-judgemental. It's also intended to inspire your own thinking rather than displace it. Only you — particularly the you of your better moments — will know which of these or others will work best for you. And to know this better, you'll need to notice more. Pay attention to which break activities help you most with which situations, adjust and iterate.

Finally, note that one of the indirect benefits of mental diversion might well be the solving of a problem you have been grappling with. Sometimes, the unfocused mind finds a path that the focused mind cannot. David Ogilvy puts it nicely (and enticingly): 'Stuff your conscious mind with information, then unhook your rational thought process. You can help this process by going for a long walk, taking a hot bath, or drinking half a pint of claret.'

For how long?

Most of the advice is to take a few minutes break every 45–60 minutes. Some data, shared widely online, suggests specifically that 52[71] minutes of work followed by 17 minutes of rest is the modus operandi of highly productive people. There are many less-cited but more substantiated studies, which indicate that 10 minutes of aerobic exercise[72] can be cognitively beneficial and that brief diversions[73] can materially help with focus.

But once again, the only truth that matters is the truth for you. You owe it to yourself to experiment and figure out what works best. Just as failing to take breaks can lead to a decline in performance, there is such a thing as taking too many breaks for too long, and we all need to find the right balance. To do so, you'll need to notice more. How short are the breaks after which you *don't* feel adequately rested? How long are the breaks after which you suspect they've been too long? Don't just choose the activities that you gravitate towards most at the start of your breaks; consider the activities that make you feel best by the end of your breaks.

I tend to take 5- or 10-minute breaks. I take 5-minute breaks from within 30-minute timeboxes (i.e. 25 minutes on the task) and 10 minutes from 60-minute timeboxes (i.e. 50 minutes on the task). I rarely need a break after a 15-minute timebox. My calendar defaults are set for 25 and 50 minutes, so setting the timeboxes with the appropriate built-in breaks is efficient and effective for me.

Outside hours

We don't just need rest from within the hustle and bustle of the day. We actually spend more time and get more of our rest outside of regular working hours, during leisure time, days off and vacations.

Just as we do for intraday breaks, we should be intentional about how we spend our leisure time, days off and vacations. Consider which purposes you'd like them to serve, be intentional and note that all three kinds of so-called outside hours can, themselves, be fruitfully timeboxed. I timebox roughly half of my outside hours.

■ ■ ■ ■

Breaks are an essential part of timeboxing. By taking our breaks well, we become more productive and less stressed. Consider the factors here and make the breaks you take your own intentional, morale- and energy-boosting respite. You are the alchemist of your experiences, responsible for blending graft, creativity, interactivity and rest into your chosen elixir.

Review

- We need breaks to rest our body and mind, and to reward achievement.

- Think broadly and proactively about what you can do in your breaks — there are many options.
- Five minutes rest for each half hour of focus is approximately the right ratio.
- Rest outside of work is also important and should also be deliberate.

Reflect

- Which activities from the table in this chapter do you think (these things are hard to measure!) help you to rest best?
- Try to think of two to three additional constructive activities not listed above.
- On a typical day, which do you find more rewarding: to rest your body or your mind? Which is more in need of rest right now?

For me, light is the signal in the transition. It's not being in the light, it's being there before it arrives. It enables me, in some sense.

— Toni Morrison

22. Better sleep

Keywords	Slumber; naps; siesta; sleep hygiene; comfort; circadian rhythm; sleep routine
Word count	1,349
Read time	7 mins

Imagine you have a mammoth, 8-hour meeting coming up. You're required for its full duration. And your performance in that meeting will have a serious impact on how you will feel for the next day and beyond. You would probably prepare carefully for such a high-stakes meeting, right? Well, we all have just such an event every single night, for which most of us prepare very little.

This book, so far, has been about the 16 or so waking hours that we split between work and leisure. That leaves 8 hours left for slumber. How can timeboxing help us with the remaining third of our daily life?

I'll make several assumptions here. I'll assume, rather than argue, that sleep is a major enabler of mood, health and productivity. I'll assume that good sleep hygiene includes (but is not limited to):

- a regular sleep schedule
- exercising earlier in the day rather than later
- judicious use of naps
- reducing or avoiding alcohol and nicotine, caffeine and other stimulants shortly before intended sleep
- managing exposure to light and, in particular, natural light through the day, evening and night

- a peaceful, comfortable environment that's dark and at the right temperature
- avoiding stimulating activities before sleep, especially worry.

There is ample and growing scientific evidence[74] for sleep hygiene.[75] The focus of this chapter, then, will be on how timeboxing can help us improve our sleep hygiene and, in turn, the quality of our sleep, mood, health and productivity.

Morning

The path to a good night's sleep starts as we wake up.

We should get some natural light soon after we wake in order to:

- Help regulate our circadian rhythm. This makes us more awake and livelier, just when we need to be, and makes it easier for us to fall asleep 16 or so hours later.
- Lift mood and energy. Natural light stimulates the production of serotonin, a neurotransmitter that regulates mood and helps us feel more alert and focused.
- Increase vitamin D levels. Exposure to sunlight is one of the primary ways our bodies produce vitamin D (which aids the health of our bones, teeth, muscles and immune system).
- Boost productivity. Natural light has also been shown to improve cognitive performance, alertness and productivity.

If you wake up when it's still dark, as Toni Morrison used to, enjoy the tranquil dark and its tender illumination. Position yourself to experience the sun's rays when they're available. If there's just no chance of that, use artificial lighting and top up with natural light when you can.

Later in the day, try to work in an environment with ready access to natural light — one study found that individuals exposed to sunlight during the day slept 46 minutes more than those in sunless work environments.[76]

Exercise in the morning (or early afternoon). People who have exercised during the day sleep better than those who don't, but physical exercising right before bedtime can adversely affect sleep.

Timebox these sleep-enhancing measures. Make sure that your first timebox of the day exposes your retinas to natural light. If your first task is to timebox your day (and I would be pleased if this were so), organize yourself so that you do it in a place of (natural) light. And timebox that morning's (or early afternoon's) exercise so that it happens, just when your body most needs it to.

Naps

Naps share many of the benefits of early natural light. Done right, they can help with mood, alertness and cognitive function. For many, the acute need they serve is to help us through a lull in our day, which often occurs in the postprandial afternoon.

There is plenty of appetite for naps. Sleeping pods are still uncommon but increasing in popularity at workplaces that seek to look after their workforce (while simultaneously maximizing their productivity, of course). And siestas, *riposinos*, *inemuris* and *wǔshuì* (all forms of daytime rest, usually taken in the afternoon) have been important practices in many cultures for centuries.

If you're able and inclined to take a nap, do it right: 20–30 minutes is the ideal length to gain the benefits without unduly affecting the remainder of your day or your sleep that night. Arrange your environment so it's conducive for sleep (see next section). You may find a guided relaxation meditation, such as yoga nidra, helps. If you are lucky enough to be able to incorporate naps into your schedule regularly, take them at roughly the same time so your body gets used to this and comes to expect it. In other words, timebox them.

Finally, experiment and discover what works for *you*. Duration, timing, music, caffeine, naps, diffusers, self-hypnosis, astral projection, what you choose to think about as you drift off and much more are all possibilities to explore.

Evening ritual

An evening sleep preparation routine will enhance the quality of your sleep.

Work backwards. When do you want to wake up? Let's say it's 7 am. So, if we assume 8 hours sleep, you'll need to get to sleep at 11 pm. Start to gradually prepare for this a couple of hours before – 9 pm in this case. That doesn't mean dedicated, exclusive devotion. But it does mean checking that a few conditions are met and abstaining from certain activities that are detrimental to good sleep.

Returning to our list of sleep hygiene factors listed above, the first three have already been discussed. Cut down on or cut out alcohol and ingested stimulants. Reduce your intake of sound with choice and volume of music or entertainment. Reduce your intake of light with a gentler, dimmer environment and a commitment to not expose your eyes to the blue light emitted by the LED screens most of us have already been glued to for much of the day (many smartphones and laptops now come with blue light settings you can adjust and schedule). Set up your sleep environment to be comfortable, noting that our bodies need to reduce in temperature in order for us to fall asleep; 18–20 degrees Celsius (64–68 Fahrenheit) is a good range for most of us. Finally, engage in restful activities at this time:

Do	Don't
• take a warm bath • have a massage • meditate • journal • listen to serene music or a tranquil podcast • calmly clear any clutter	• watch a horror film • play video games • eat a big meal • engage in an adversarial conversation • take a look at your inbox and get lured into a spiral of work thoughts

Practically speaking, you'll achieve 90% of the benefits of the above simply by eliminating screens from the last hour or two of your waking day. Timeboxing can also serve to *prevent* the doing of a thing for a specified period and this deliberate deprivation is an important behaviour to habitualize — 90% of us fail at it.[77]

Finally, notice that much of the advice here also applies to those around you. Kids, partners, flatmates and others might also benefit from some of these practices. To the extent that you can influence them, do. The poor sleep of others in your immediate vicinity might very well impinge on yours. Besides, it's good to be kind.

Good sleep leads to better mood, health and productivity. Good sleep hygiene leads to good sleep. And the timeboxing of certain behaviours and activities leads to good sleep hygiene. Ergo, timebox your sleep routine.

Review

- Good sleep is crucial for mood, health and productivity.
- Sleep hygiene involves taking common-sense steps to improve the quality of sleep.
- So, timebox measures to improve sleep hygiene, such as early morning exposure to natural light, exercise, limited naps and evening sleep preparation (reducing noise and light, calm activities, no screens).
- These practices can benefit those around us too.

Reflection

- Timebox some recurring daylight and exercise into your calendar for tomorrow, now.
- How is your sleep hygiene? Write down the positive and negative practices you commonly engage in. Which extra good behaviours could you add? Which bad behaviours could you eliminate?
- What's one thing you could do right now to eliminate a bad sleep hygiene practice?
- Partly in preparation for the next chapter and partly to

encourage you to consider the broad array of sleep aids now on offer, what technology do you have that could be used to enhance your sleep? Apps (sleep trackers, breathing, guided meditation), wearable sleep trackers (rings, watches), Bluetooth eye masks, smart mattresses, weighted blankets and, for real connoisseurs, neurofeedback and EEG devices.

*Technology is a useful servant
but a dangerous master.*

— Christian Lous Lange

23. Tools & tech

Keywords	Hardware; software; features; digital; analogue; metacognition
Word count	1,421
Read time	7 mins

The printed version of this chapter won't age well. So, I'll keep an online version of it updated at www.marczaosanders.com/tech.

Technological advancement, in general as well as that pertaining specifically to timeboxing, is relentless. Over the past couple of years, start-ups have produced many new apps to assist with calendars, to-do lists and timeboxing. In parallel, the world's largest tech companies have released several features with the same ends in mind.

Still, I contend that most of us don't need many tools, tech or features to realize the substantive benefits of timeboxing. I just use a digital calendar and a document for my notes (which doubles up as a to-do list).

But everyone's different and certain digital, physical or mental tools may be of use to *you*. I urge you to think about the purpose of, and your need for, such tools. Is it to time, to remind, to order, to share, to sync or something else? Are you sure you can't do that adequately with the basics?

Digital

Clock

You'll need to keep the time, obviously. If you're working on a computer, which so many of us do for most of our working day, you'll have constant sight of the time (usually in the bottom- or top-right corner of your screen). This is a much better way of keeping track of the time than a smartphone, which comes with a lot of distracting baggage. A portable timepiece such as a wristwatch also, obviously, serves this purpose but you've probably got it covered already. In general, beware of any interface that is also a portal into dozens of worlds you don't need to be in.

Apps

Much investment has gone into productivity, time management and even, specifically, timeboxing apps over the last few years. Search online for 'timeboxing app', and many will appear. This certainly supports the notion, argued for in this book, that there is a demand for greater control and intentionality in our lives. But is an app an effective way of achieving this? One of the main advantages of using an app over proactively managing a digital calendar yourself is that if the schedule changes, the app can automatically reorganize the calendar. Of course, schedules do change. But in over a decade of timeboxing, I've never found the manual reorganization of my day to be a problem for myself or anyone else. Indeed, the fact I need to pay attention and decide myself where to now fit my appointments in light of some change helps me process what they are and when they need to happen in the context of my life; handing over this authority to AI-powered automation would diminish my awareness, agency and performance. There is also a raft of new to-do apps and calendar apps with various overlapping functionality, which may be vulnerable to the same criticism. Nonetheless, I do recommend trying some of them out. At worst, you'll remove the app in a few days' time. At best, you'll have a tool that makes timeboxing a consistent reality for you. Or perhaps, in between the best- and worst-case scenarios, you'll pick up a timeboxing trick that hadn't occurred to you (or to me).

Features within digital calendars

Microsoft To Do, a task management app, touches on most of the features of timeboxing. Microsoft also recently made it possible to drag an email onto the calendar icon to create a timebox for it, complete with the email's text. Google's Focus Time is intended to help users avoid distractions. Over the past year, Google also rolled out Time Insights, which provides analytics on how users spend their time. Of these, as I mentioned in Chapter 11, I only use Time Insights to monitor and manage how I spend time on the different areas of my life. Investigate these and other such features. Since you're almost certainly using a digital calendar anyway, there's not much extra hassle or cost in utilizing a new native feature.

Large Language Models (LLMs)

ChatGPT is, as of this writing, the fastest-growing consumer app of all time. Although it and other LLMs are not specifically designed for timeboxing, they do have a particular application here. One of the themes in this book is that our performance of a task is usually significantly enhanced when we've had time to prepare for it — if our brains have been primed for it. I advocate making timeboxes specifically for the preparation of meetings, in order to set off the cognitive whirrings that help us complete the task well. And for many tasks, LLMs can accelerate that cognitive whirring by generating ideas, summarizing relevant text, finding reference materials and combining concepts. These can be used in a preparatory timebox or in the timebox itself to kick-start your own thinking on a topic. In this context and to this end, their assistance to humanity is clear and pure and safe. I'll leave the debate about existential threats and other abominable possibilities to others.

Physical

You don't need any physical tools but you might like some.

Calendars, notebooks and to-do lists come in paper as well as digital form. For many, there's something satisfying about seeing, touching, feeling and even smelling an object in the real world. For others, the benefits of backing up to the cloud, syncing devices and sharing with others far outweigh those of antiquated, analogue methods. I'm mostly in the latter camp, at least as regards what's needed for timeboxing.

But even die-hard digitalists should think about how to make the physical world help rather than hinder their timeboxing routine. We need the objects around us to help keep us focused on the timebox we're in. Such physical objects might be very low-tech, but they're still tech.[78] An hourglass, for example, might be an effective means of both keeping track of how much time you have left for a task and also a reminder of the very fact that you are timeboxing and to return to the timebox if and when you get sidetracked. I have a cherished hourglass, which I have used since I was 30. A Post-it note with a mantra like 'Return to Calendar' might serve this latter purpose too. There are cube timers (these are in fact both digital and physical), often with units of 15, 20, 30 and 60 minutes (note that these happen to align closely to the standard timebox sizes I proposed in Chapter 12), which may appeal to some.

Mental

Metacognitive skills are essential tools for timeboxing. While digital technology and physical tools can and should be used to reduce distraction, retain focus and escape rabbit holes, we can't escape our own minds. Thoughts will intrude, however many digital and physical barriers we put up. Our only recourse is to get better at noticing when this happens and coming back to the calendar and specifically the timebox we're in, as emphasized in Chapter 18.

Recall that it's possible to develop our own sense of time. We all have our circadian rhythm and an internal clock. We can develop our sense of how long we've taken on a timeboxed task and, with practice, reduce our need to clock-watch (itself a distraction). Timeboxing improves timekeeping, and vice versa.

■ ■ ■ ■

You'll get most of the benefits of timeboxing with the essentials described in the other chapters of this book. But some optional extras might just have a positive effect on your joy of timeboxing. So, consider them properly, note that they may come from the digital, physical or mental realms, and be clear on what purpose they will serve. After all, we want timeboxing to work, don't we?

Choosing how to spend our time on earth — the only conscious experience we can count on — is fundamental for us all. Timeboxing is a good, and in my view the very best, way to achieve this. So, do it daily, do it well and do it in your own way.

Review

- There are many tools and features that can be used to timebox.
- You don't need any technology to timebox successfully.
- But some of them might enhance your experience.
- Think about which tools might help you and what purpose they would serve.

Reflect

- On which tools and technologies does your system of personal productivity depend? List them and examine them. How might you improve that system?
- Download a timeboxing app now and try it for a week.
- I've described timeboxing as both a mindset and a method. How would you describe the mindset element of timeboxing? And the method?

But now my task is smoothly done:
I can fly, or I can run.

— John Milton

24. It's working

Keywords	Behaviour change; benefits; objections; adopt; adapt; embed; own; customize
Word count	1,962
Read time	10 mins

The question is not whether timeboxing works; it does (see *Chapter 2 — It works*). The question is whether it's working *for you*. If you've followed the learning-by-doing through the journey so far, it should be working. But let's try to be more certain. So, what would it mean for timeboxing to be working for you? It would mean that you are:

- timeboxing, habitually
- thinking clearly about what you should do
- getting those things done when you say you would
- realizing some of timeboxing's many benefits
- making the mindset and method your own.

If all of this is happening, I'm sure you'll be feeling good about the method and wanting to continue. But if there's even one gap, you may be missing out. Some of the questions posed in this chapter will help pinpoint and troubleshoot any issues you are having.

But first, let's adjust our expectations.

Don't expect timeboxing to work 24/7

I don't timebox my whole life. There are many contexts in which timeboxing is impractical, even a nuisance. By developing a sense of what and when these are, we'll know when to *not* expect to be able to timebox, thereby avoiding unnecessary, inevitable failure.

Some periods of work and home life are inherently unpredictable. For example, you're going to an event bursting with serendipitous possibilities (a festival, a party, a conference, a barbecue) — a lot will happen, but when, where and with whom are impossible to predict or control. Or you're about to be assailed by your kids, full of indefatigable energy and enthusiasm. Or you're undertaking a home renovation and have a day of deliveries and questions from suppliers and workpeople. For all of these kinds of situations, timeboxing with any level of intraday granularity is likely to be unproductive.

Work that is substantially predictable and structured may not be as suitable for timeboxing. Many occupations, like those of factory workers, cashiers, food service employees and security guards, offer limited opportunities for prioritization within the workday. For individuals in such roles, timeboxing might therefore have limited utility during working hours. However, outside of work — leisure and sleep constitute approximately two-thirds of life — the benefits of timeboxing remain substantial.

Do you want more spontaneity in your life? Timeboxing is not, on the face of it, an obvious method of achieving that. And there are certain benefits to disorder: variety, surprise, challenge, creativity, problem-solving and so on. (But, even then, there may be timeboxable activities that enable *second-order spontaneity*: doing nothing;[79] doing something random; being in a place [a bar, art gallery, dance hall] where spontaneity thrives; or taking part in an activity [an improv class, a conversation with a stranger on a commute, a creative writing class] where spontaneity thrives.)

Finally, don't let timeboxing spoil the party. Explicitly determined end points can suppress surprise and curtail fun. When you know from the start of the evening that you'll be leaving the ball at exactly midnight . . . it's not such a good ball.

Are you doing it? Is it working?

These are two importantly distinct questions. Doing = behaviour; working = benefit. Notice that the worst possible outcome would be that you *are* doing it but that it's *not* working — you're making the effort but not achieving the benefit. So, let's establish how you're getting on. Answer the questions below as accurately as you can.

Are you doing it?

Question	Answer options (choose one)		
Do you usually timebox most of your day ahead of time (either the morning or evening before)?	Yes		No
Do you prepare your environment to be distraction-free and conducive to work?	Yes	Sometimes	No
Do you maintain a to-do list methodically?	Yes	Somewhat	No
Does your to-do list routinely feed your timeboxes?	Yes	Sometimes	No
Do you choose when to reply to emails?	Yes	Sometimes	No
Do your timeboxes make sense when you get to them?	Yes	Sometimes	No
Do you usually finish your tasks within the timebox?	Yes	Sometimes	No

Do you aim to get something done, shipped and shared?	Yes	Sometimes	No
Do you successfully come back from daydreams and rabbit holes to your calendar?	Yes	Sometimes	No
Are you good at estimating the size of timeboxes?	Yes	Sometimes	No
Do you actively think about when and how to take breaks?	Yes	Sometimes	No
Do you keep a sleep routine?	Yes	Sometimes	No

Is it working?

Question	Answer options (choose one)		
Do you associate timeboxing with a particular, significant benefit to your life?	Yes		No
Have you found a use for having your timeboxes recorded, historically?	Yes		No
Do you feel less stressed as a result of a timeboxed, one-thing-at-a time approach?	Yes	Somewhat	No
Do you think more clearly, deeper or better?	Yes	Sometimes	No
Have colleagues benefitted from being able to see your schedule?	Yes	Sometimes	No
Have you benefitted from seeing theirs?	Yes	Sometimes	No
Are you getting more done?	Yes	Sometimes	No
Are you sleeping better?	Yes	Sometimes	No

Have you used the practice to adapt, at all, the arc of your life?	Yes		No
Have you identified the most important segments of your life?	Yes		No
Do you now have a sense of how much time you spend on each of these?	Yes	Somewhat	No
How often do you not follow through with a scheduled timebox?	Rarely	Sometimes	Frequently
Do you believe timeboxing works?	Yes	A little bit	No

Between the two tables, if you have 12 or so answers in the left-hand column, you're doing well.

There's a shortcut to knowing it's working. You may have already used timeboxing to do something immeasurably special — to reconnect with an old friend, deepen a skill, truly immerse yourself in play with a child, re-establish regular devoted time with a partner. If you have, you won't need me or a quiz to tell you it's working. If you have, you will know the true power of the practice.

Possible headwinds

Soon (likely in less than 10 minutes), you will finish reading this book. Life will flood back in. You'll get busy. Not everyone who tries it sticks with it.

So, before we leave each other, let's anticipate the most common pitfalls. I've sourced and prioritized the below from my own experience, in discussions with other timeboxing adherents and adversaries, as well as in online forums.

Urgent tasks just come up, throwing my timeboxes into disarray.

There are some occupations that are necessarily and constantly at the mercy of chance events. If you work as a nurse or doctor in an A&E ward, any premeditated plans would be cast aside and so timeboxing wouldn't work. Timeboxing is not advisable for emergency workers (at least not during their working lives). And although most of us don't operate in such an extreme, unpredictable environment, many of us have intermittent bouts of high urgency: an important customer calls, a press opportunity arises, a boss makes an unexpected demand. But such eventualities neither invalidate nor undermine timeboxing. First, these periods of uncertainty are, for most of us, the exception rather than the rule. Second, when urgent requests are likely, our response should be to timebox the checking and processing of messages *more frequently* (every 2 hours, say), rather than not at all. Third, priorities do change, timeboxes are not set in stone and we all can, will and should adapt them, from time to time. (See *Chapter 13 — Box-ordering*.)

You're overwhelmed by the planning — you feel like you're losing time and not getting to the actual task at hand.

Once you have a little practice, it takes just 15 minutes to timebox a whole day of tasks. Fifteen minutes to facilitate the following 15 hours is a steal. (See *Chapter 9 — The basics*.)

You don't see it through. You've set the timeboxes, they're in your calendar, but you're just not getting them done.

Make sure you're picking the right kind of task for the frame of mind you're in. Know that it's just one thing that you're asking of yourself. Start with the very smallest act to get you moving in the right direction. And see *Chapter 18 — Rabbit holes & other distractions* and *Chapter 19 — Build the habit*.

You don't finish on time.

First, be reassured that scientific and other evidence suggests that this should work (*Chapter 2 — It works*). Are you estimating tasks realistically? (*Chapter 12 — Box-sizing*) Are you pacing and racing your way through your timeboxes? (*Chapter 16 — Pacing & racing*) Do you have a strong, workable concept of good enough? (*Chapter 17 — Ship something*) With experience and perseverance, these can all be fine-tuned to achieve a productive harmony and get you finished on time, consistently.

A big idea

Identify one big timeboxing idea that you truly, viscerally believe in and the method and mindset are far more likely to stay with you. It may be that you have already picked such a concept out and hold it dear. If you haven't, consider these:

- **Agency.** Timeboxing is about determining the tiny handful of things we want to influence out of the universe of stuff we can't, and influencing just those. We really can't control outputs and outcomes. We can only decide what we do and when we do it. This is both humbling and empowering.
- **Higher power.** Whether we're religious or not, there are times when many of us feel we'd like ready access to a reassuring higher power. Timeboxing provides exactly that; the higher power is ourself, in an earlier, better moment.

- **Meta-habit.** Timeboxing is the one habit to rule them all, a precious meta-habit that can bring as many other valuable habits as you can fit into a calendar.
- **100% more productive.** We saw, back in *Chapter 7 — For productivity*, that there's plenty of evidence that the method doubles our productivity.

■ ■ ■ ■

Adopting and adapting a new behaviour doesn't happen overnight. I continue to hone the skill through my second decade of timeboxing. I now timebox considerably more than I did at first, because it's worked so well for me (I score 21 on the table above, btw).

This is a book. It contains cutting-edge research and practice on the subject of timeboxing at the time of publication. But as with any discipline, further ideas, tactics and tools will occur or emerge over time. Sign up to the newsletter (called *One Thing at a Time*) at www.marczaosanders.com/newsletter to have these arrive, weekly, in your inbox. They will remind you of some of the salient points from this book and help you to course correct, if and when needed. It's also a means of being in touch with me and others who timebox.

For me, choosing what we do with our time is all there is. Timeboxing is the best method I've encountered or can conceive of to help us make the most of this privilege, to choose a life we will cherish.

Review

- Timeboxing won't work in certain situations, and it pays to know which these are.
- Develop a sense both of how much you're doing it and what benefits it's bringing you.
- Brace yourself for the obstacles you will meet while adopting this new behaviour.
- There are some big ideas associated with the practice of timeboxing; I've picked out four here but you may have thoughts of your own.

Reflect

- Answer all the questions in the two tables in this chapter.
- Send a scheduled email (most email services now provide this feature) to your future self in three months' time to answer these same questions again. Keep a record of how you answer them now (write 'X items in left-column' in the email you send), so you can compare and measure progress.
- Which of the big timeboxing ideas in this chapter feels most important to you? Or is there some other idea that means even more?

Epilogue

Artificial Intelligence (AI) & writing

Just before I signed the book deal (February 2023), Artificial Intelligence was capturing the mainstream public's imagination. This new breed of AI, in the form of Large Language Models (LLMs), could write and think, apparently. ChatGPT in particular became the fastest consumer app to reach 100 million users.[80] Suddenly, there was a new intelligence in town, smarter than us in many respects. Humankind's dominance of the planet, predicated almost entirely on our intelligence, was threatened. How would this pan out?

Some experts predict that the rise of the LLMs spells the start of the end for writing and publishing. Certainly, the new technology can perform astonishing feats. It can piece together cohesive content on almost any topic in a flash, a capability well beyond even our most celebrated mortal writers. It's natural, then, to infer that AI has matched or surpassed human writing already, or that it will do so soon.

This inference is natural but mistaken, I think. Speed, encyclopedic knowledge, prolificacy, 24/7 availability and surface-level cogency bring many breathtaking advantages. But they are not yet a substitute for the deep thought, broad contextual assimilation, complex emotional understanding and sheer brilliance that humans, at their best, are capable of. Our jaws dropped as we watched AI articulate perfect sentences and paragraphs in a split second. But when we stay with it over the course of several pages, those jaws gradually close, attentions wander, and we take our breath back.

For now, at least as I write in the Autumn / Fall of 2023, human capability is above that of machines for original, creative thinking and writing.

Timeboxing to write

I timeboxed every single one of the efforts that went into this book. I have a record in my digital calendar of all the timeboxes for the initial pitch, the drafts, the edits, the meetings, the real-world stories, the epigraphs, permissions, illustrations, acknowledgements, this epilogue, and much else.

More specifically, the method was this. I had 24 chapters to write in 24 weeks — roughly a 1,800-word chapter a week. I kept a live document with the plan for each of those chapters and would add ideas to the appropriate section, whenever they occurred. On Monday evenings, after work, I'd take a look at the plan and notes I had and spend exactly 60 minutes thinking up new angles, references and lines of research. I'd then give my subconscious three nights' sleep and on the Thursday evening I'd spend another hour preparing a detailed plan for the chapter in the form of structured bullet points. Two more sleeps later, early on Saturday mornings, I'd be ready to write the three or four sections of the chapter, each in 15- or 30-minute timeboxed bursts, which, with my own reviews and editing, took 3-4 hours in total. I'd then invariably go for a midmorning run, during which a couple more ideas would often come to mind, and incorporate those in a final 30-minute edit. And that would be another chapter draft done. The key lesson is that I never sat down to write a chapter cold.

As I got into my stride, and as I took some time off work, I could get two or three chapters written in a single week. In the end, the 45,000-word first draft of the book took four intense months. Finishing several months early was welcome news to the publishers, as well as a satisfying meta-vindication of timeboxing.

So, you have in your hands (or in your ears if you're listening to the audiobook) proof that timeboxing works for me. For you, the ultimate proof of the practice lies in what *you* do with it, and when.

Timeless

Other than *Chapter 23 — Tools & tech*, the subject matter of this book should age well.

I discovered recently, a while after I'd finished the book, that the word 'time' is the most frequently used noun in the English language. This has been the case since at least 2006.[81] It's a major theme in many poems, films, songs, blogs, books and much more. We use it and read it once every 500 words — every two pages. Usage of the word is a little above that level in this particular book.

The logic of timeboxing is sound. Deciding what's important, when it needs to be done, and doing it (and nothing else) is hard to argue with. This plight and privilege isn't going away. It's really all there is for us. And it's plenty.

I believe time and timeboxing are keepers.

Acknowledgements

This book incorporates a lot of what's most important to me in life — kindness, thinking, openness, light-heartedness, communication, agency. So, the influences on the book are the influences on my life, and innumerable. I'll confine the gratitude expressed here to those that most directly helped to write *Timeboxing*. I'll go around the room in chronological order.

I thank Helen Zao, my mum, both first and foremost. For giving me life, of course, but more for everything since, including, to take a small sample, teaching me to write, introducing me to good writing, inspiring me to think differently by always doing so herself, for ginger tea and conversations, for a wonderful sister, and for life-long friendship. Also, specifically, for the tireless editing of this book.

My sister, Sibyl, for accepting my first lesson about time, and for her unwavering love, support, advice and fun 👍.

Mr Dorian, an unforgettable teacher who helped me to see language and literature — from Shakespeare to Tennessee Williams to Ian McEwan — in higher resolution. It's incalculable, the good a good teacher does.

I am blessed with friends who have given me ideas and experiences that have helped with this book, directly and indirectly. Rich and Rob, for the finest of excursions, discussions and meditations. Fosterman, for the nest in which Part Two was hatched. Jimbo for paying the price up front, a timeboxing concept, ultimately. José, for the encouragement to think and write and lead grown-up, corporate audiences, and also for the idea of our first self, our higher power. Greg, for the unprecedented and almost entirely welcome intellectual challenge over the years on AI, learning and timeboxing. Albion, for the shared thoughts and the confidence that I could 'definitely write a book'. Stephen, for simplicity and straightforwardness — they've been a guide for me ever since I heard it from you. Peter, for your very uncorporate encouragement. Manto, for the same. Tamsin, for your off-beat originality, and for gently imbuing me with social media bravery. And to Julie for the ⚓ when I needed it.

I'm also lucky to have friends with a hand (or more) in the world of writing. Ed, thank you for leading the way, for material help when I needed it, and the dice. Patrick, thanks for your own literary trailblazing, for adventures, and for Jim (see below). Anna for the courage and spirit (👻) to cross genres. Jenny for Xmas homework, Chinese, and your warm, first-person plural approach.

My family has helped me and the book every day for almost a year. Luka, your pride kept the fire of writing burning through difficult moments. Aya, thank you for early-morning edits and helping me ask the right questions. Favian, your easy-going nature helps me to keep timeboxing itself in check. Ksush, for the demonstration that batty brilliance is an alternative to conscientious timekeeping. Mattia for the patience and *riposinos*. Olya and Dave for wisdom and support, notably in Costa Rica. Sam for 6zero, our first-time project. Marlowe for your 'brilliant' book review in the park. My wife, Lola, for your inspiring, free spirit and spontaneity, your love, your positive reviews of the drafts, and a very gradual embrace of the practice I think I'm starting to see.

Thanks to the Filtered team and Board (past and present) for giving me the space to write this book and for many of the experiences that underpin it. The interactions with you over the years have helped hone much of the material here. A special mention here to my co-founders, Vin and Chris, with whom I've been through so much and whose thinking has shaped mine a great deal. Ditto Toby (who's not far off co-founder too) for the Zen, the 🖨 and being, like me, a student and teacher of timeboxing.

Dana from *Harvard Business Review*, thank you for taking a punt on a Timeboxing piece some years ago and for your expert and consistently cheerful interactions ever since. You are a joy to work with.

My literary agent, Jim Gill from United Agents, has fought my corner with loyalty, grit, humour and results. And to Amber Garvey, also at United, for being a rock throughout this process.

To my new friends at Penguin Random House in the UK. First, Karolina for the enterprise and tenacity in seeking me out and making this book come to be and for being a resilient sounding board for my ideas — good, bad and odd. To Paula for helping make this book about life more than business, as it should be. To Emma for taking such a positive attitude and energy to many last-minute edits. And there are many others at Penguin who helped put the book together and bring it to many, many countries.

To my even newer friends at St Martin's Press in the US. The team there are all excellent, but I must mention Tim Bartlett, whose detailed, meticulous editing and care made the book substantially better (and two chapters shorter) than it would otherwise be.

I'd like to thank some established authors, Kim Scott, Luke Burgis, Karie Willyerd, who have been generous with their precious time and valuable advice. I will try to follow your lead and be as nice and useful to new authors.

A special thanks to BJ Fogg. For leading the way in the field of habit-forming by encouraging millions to make them tiny and easy. For your generous, reassuring review of this book. And for coaching me through Chapter 19. Mahalo!

Thanks to the timeboxers from around the world who contributed their stories. I approached lots of people online who had said something about timeboxing, not expecting to get more than a handful of responses. In fact, I got many dozens. This strand of the work reminded me of how positive and lovely human connection, even between unfamiliar people on vast digital social media platforms, can sometimes be. I'm sorry that not all the stories can be used here but I can say that the part that all of you played is greater than you might know.

The last person to thank, in this chronological order, is you, the reader. Thank you for making an effort to reconsider how you use your time. In that hope and aspiration, at least, we share a bond.

One hot summer afternoon, two girls, Lorina and her little sister Alice, were sitting together on a riverbank. Lorina was reading to Alice. Alice, bored by the pictureless, conversationless book, fell into a wondrous, dream-filled slumber. Minutes later she awoke, hungry, and scuttled off to tea. But Lorina stayed out, enjoying the hazy summer hum of the murmuring water and buzzing insects. She wandered aimlessly from the bank and discovered a sun-kissed, bricked pathway, which led to an unfamiliar garden, and into an unfamiliar house. No one around. In the hallway, an hourglass shows 24 hours to go. She looks again; it says 13. Something's wrong. Her heart pounds. She goes back outside, hurrying now, unsure which way. She follows the long shadows of the wood, brushing past tall grass and flickering fireflies. She trips on a tree root and falls down a very deep hole.

It's pitch-black at the bottom. Her hands feel a rough, earthy surface above, below and on each side. It's a tunnel, but somehow askew. She gets to her feet and stoops forward, but her legs won't move as she means them to. So many turnings. Up, up, down, down, left, right, left, right, back, start, stop. She's breathless and dizzy. Out of the corner of her eye, there's movement – a small animal. A duck? A rabbit? She gives chase and then all of a sudden, the overhanging surface she's been struggling under opens up into a vast underground cavern: a hippodrome with a racecourse. A crowd of fantastical spectators cheers on the runners: a rabbit (or is it a hare?), a tortoise, a Greek warrior. The tortoise is in the lead, yet somehow the slowest of the three. It's impossible to tell who will win. Lorina peers closer, but she can't tell one moment apart from the next, or whether the moments are even separate at all. A sense of in-betweenness engulfs her and spirits her up through the layers of earth and rock, into another wood. Only this one is completely silent – no wildlife, no wind, yet rich as plumcake. Lying on the grass right by her is a red book. Then she has it! It's the very book, *Return to Raceland*, she was reading to her sister that afternoon. It's open at page 217. Rejoin there or venture further at marczaosanders.com/rabbit-hole.

Timeboxing stories from around the world

> **"** The main benefit of timeboxing for me is that it helps me set realistic priorities and stick to them. A simple to-do list doesn't include how much time everything takes, so it would be easy for me to overextend myself and then feel bad about it. With timeboxing, I can see exactly how much time I have in a day and allocate it as needed. If there's too much to fit in a day, then I know it's time to reassess my priorities.
>
> — Fatemeh Fakhraie, Marketing Manager, Northwest Community Credit Union, Eugene, Oregon, USA

As a busy freelancer managing multiple clients and projects, I'd find it very difficult to efficiently run my business without timeboxing. After leaving my last office job more than 6 years ago, I realised pretty quickly that my to-do list was just never getting done. I needed to come up with a better way of managing my time, so I started allocating a specific timeslot to a specific task — not realising there was a name for what I was doing until quite recently! I'm a big advocate of 'distraction-free working' — I will often have my mobile phone turned off when I'm in work-mode. The combination of that, and timeboxing, is priceless.

— Tamsin Isaacs, Founder, Know Good Social, Barcelona, Spain

I used to work for a big software company where I was head of several units. Keeping a record of what happened during a crisis or an incident has been really helpful just to remember what happened in case I am asked questions or to justify the decisions I took. There are so many balls in the air and it's just impossible to remember everything so I used timeboxing for this.

— Nadia Gicqueau-Ryan MBA, Business Change, Flexibility & Transformation leader, Paris, France

" Timeboxing is a simple, effective practice that can be used to optimize cognitive performance by aligning what we call overarching states of mind (SoM) with corresponding activities. By allocating fixed time periods (boxes) for specific tasks, we can take steps to intentionally match the task with the right SoM, reducing friction and increasing ease and productivity. For example, suppose we need to brainstorm some ideas for a sales presentation. If we recognize that this task is about creativity, deep thinking, open-mindedness and collaboration, we can and should prepare for it differently and deliberately: collate the relevant information, remove distractions, remind ourselves of the need to be open-minded and actively listen, remove critical thinking from the room, and make sure mood is upbeat. (The link between mood and creativity is provocative yet by now well-established.)

By aligning activities with the right SoM for those activities, individuals can unlock their full cognitive potential and accomplish tasks with greater precision, effectiveness and sense of fulfilment.

— Professor Moshe Bar, internationally renowned cognitive neuroscientist and author of *Mindwandering: How Your Constant Mental Drift Can Improve Your Mood and Boost Your Creativity*, Tel-Aviv, Israel

" The main benefit of using timeboxing — and something that's now helping my career — is that I can place any actions from my ever-growing to-do list into my own high-priority filing cabinet: my calendar. I can then relax, knowing it's waiting for me when it needs my attention.

For example, if I know something is or isn't urgent but still needs addressing at some point, I place it in my calendar knowing confidently that I will get to the subject/task when the time comes. With so many plates to spin these days, timeboxing helps me relax.

However, it's not just about work. Timeboxing also allows me and my team to add other important life events such as self-managed learning, reflection, time with my kids and family, lunch, housework (the joys!), even walking the dog!

— Lee Wardman, BDR Manager EMEA for Horizons, Durham, UK

Timeboxing is all about the act of doing, which is why for those who allow their fear of how long to timebox for to stop them, my advice is to just start. Treat it as a test with you as your own baseline and start with a task that you would classify as low risk. Afterwards, take a moment to reflect on the experience and make the commitment to yourself to learn from it and use those learnings to help inform the next time you timebox. This exercise is about committing to yourself through finding balance. Don't let your fear of perfectionism stop you from bettering yourself.

— Jenna Drapkin, VP, Global Client Success, Degreed, New York City, USA.

I run a growing yoga/fitness business in a major city and timeboxing has been a vital tool for managing our lessons across multiple practice rooms. This approach not only helps in coordinating classes and ensuring consistent coaching of instructors. Many of our yoga clients have shared that incorporating timeboxing, especially scheduling early morning yoga sessions, has uplifted their energy levels and focus throughout the days — at home and at work.

The harmony and success I enjoy in both my professional and personal life is deeply connected to the benefits of timeboxing.

— Bada Ding, 丁蔚雯, Owner of Soft Yoga Studios, Jinjiang, Chengdu City, China

Set deadlines for the important. When you have a project related to business development that's important but not urgent, it's easy for it to get pushed off for weeks or even months. Put in place some type of deadlines so that the project is forced to be a priority instead of always being deferred. **Break down projects.** Large endeavors that have a multitude of steps over time should not only have one final deadline but also intermediate deadlines along the way. This helps avoid procrastination and allows everyone to adjust their expectations if certain elements take longer than expected.

— Elizabeth Grace Saunders, time management coach and author, Ann Arbor, Michigan, USA

As a new parent, co-founding a growing company, timeboxing has become a very important aspect of my life. Between coverage for our baby and prioritizing family time/meals, I know that I have to fix my work/creativity/computer activities in timeboxed windows on my calendar.

These boundaries are rather helpful because they let me know that if I'm going to get stuff done, it needs to get done in those windows. It motivates me tremendously to know that if I don't finish it in time, within the set window, then there will be a knock-on effect for subsequent items.

— Adam Fishman, Co-Founder of Onora, Boston, USA

" It is relatively easy as a designer to get trapped in endless tweaking cycles whilst in pursuit of that elusive conceptual perfection. Having said that, after nearly a decade crafting luxury tech products for the high-end fashion world, I've learned that dynamic timeboxing is key for fast, efficient work. In this volatile industry, long production cycles just don't cut it and reactivity is as crucial as proactivity. Rather than static time limits, I use variable shifting timeboxes based on the project's constraints and evolving needs. This flexible approach ensures I'm prioritizing and focusing on the right things at the right time.

Our studio executes swiftly, adopting a continuous collaborative process of draft designs to internally align the team so that we can ship products fast that still capture the full essence of our vision. Details are refined at a later stage through rapid iterations driven by client feedback. Luxury demands perfection, yes, but also values speed and novelty. With dynamic timeboxes, we deliver both and seize fleeting trends while still upholding uncompromising quality standards. Float like a butterfly, ship like a bee!

— Daniel Lazzari, Executive Art Director, Bressan Design Studio, Milan, Italy

In the bustling realm of prototype product design in China, maintaining mental clarity can be difficult. Timeboxing, in my experience, has been the bridge between efficiency and mindfulness.

In our innovative workspace, the whirlwind of projects and deadlines can easily overwhelm. But timeboxing allows us to segment tasks, bringing focus to the present moment. This approach does more than streamline work; it settles the nerves and centers the mind. Just as mindfulness teaches us to be present, timeboxing channels our energy to the task at hand, reducing scattered thoughts and the anxieties they bring.

— Zhang Chi-Yang 张驰洋 , Owner of The AA Bookstore, Chengdu, China

I use timeboxing to stay focused and productive. I timebox my work on emails to two 60-minute slots during the day, so that I can avoid interruptions during meetings. I also timebox activities that are important for my well-being, such as strength training for 30 minutes right after waking up and running before the start of the day. This helps me to stay well-rested, healthy and energized, which enables me to be more effective in my work.

— Lapo Mori, Partner at McKinsey & Company, Denver, Colorado, USA

" Timeboxing has revolutionized the way I approach my work week, providing me with a structured and consistent framework for managing my time effectively. By implementing timeboxing, I have experienced significant improvements in my productivity, reduced pressure, and a heightened focus on the most critical value-adding tasks. The benefits of timeboxing are not limited to my own experience; my team has also embraced this approach, resulting in noticeable enhancements in our collective efficiency.

We are a globally dispersed talent team with members in Canada, Senegal, Ghana, Rwanda, Uganda, Kenya, and South Africa, and at times faced challenges of longer working days in an attempt to address the high volume of recruitment activities. Calendars were not always visible to all team members or other colleagues in the organization, which would at times result in double booked or overlapping meetings. Traditional to-do lists had some gaps in addressing these issues. However, digitally enabled timeboxing using our shared Outlook calendars has emerged as a valuable solution, enabling us to prioritize tasks, gain clarity on our objectives, and allocate specific time slots for completing important activities.

— Carol Hondonga, Global Director Talent, Mastercard Foundation, Kigali City, Rwanda

" I have a **shared calendar** and sync work and personal calendars with my wife. I have a series of **immovable weekly blocks** for recurrent activities. Daily: morning 15 minutes yoga + 30 minutes workout, checking news and socials, time with kids. Weekly: writing summaries and newsletter, doing illustrations, lunch with my wife, and one activity with the kids

If something unexpected arises, I move the timebox. For example, if I can't check my articles in the early morning one day, I know that I need 30 minutes, and I'll pick the next available time.

I also have a **Todoist list** of other things that I want to do during the week but have no specific commitment for. So when there's time, I pick one of these and work on that for 30 to 60 minutes. I take a **5–10 minute break** after 30 to 60 minutes, depending on the task — usually a walk to the kitchen or outside.

When doing **focused work**, I keep my mobile in another room to increase friction when I feel the urge to pick it up. And I leave my mobile **'sleeping' in a closet** from 19:00, focusing only on my kids. I don't pick it up until the following day at 5:00. On top of these, kids, work, and especially self-distractions, come into play, and so it's still by no means a 'perfectly controlled' life. 😊

— Roberto Ferraro, Integration Director, CaixaBank, Barcelona, Spain

Notes

1   Daniel Markovitz, 'To-Do Lists Don't Work', Harvard Business Review, 2012 https://hbr.org/2012/01/to-do-lists-dont-work

2   Marc Zao-Sanders, 'How Timeboxing Works and Why It Will Make You More Productive', Harvard Business Review, 2018 https://hbr.org/2018/12/how-timeboxing-works-and-why-it-will-make-you-more-productive

3   https://www.tiktok.com/@timeboxmedia

4   Grant A. Pignatiello, et al., 'Decision Fatigue: A Conceptual Analysis', J Health Psychol, 2018 https://www.ncbi.nlm.nih.gov/pmc/articles/PMC6119549/

5   www.filtered.com

6   Aldous Huxley argues in this video from 1958 that technology and population growth together curtail freedom: https://www.youtube.com/watch?v=alasBxZsb40

7   Immanuel Kant, *Groundwork of the Metaphysics of Morals*, 1785

8   Brian Tracy, 'Eat That Frog, Explained by Brian Tracy', Brian Tracy International https://www.briantracy.com/blog/time-management/the-truth-about-frogs/

9   All but delegating and using technology.

10 Peter M. Gollwitzer, 'Implementation Intentions: Strong Effects of Simple Plans', American Psychologist, 1999 https://doi.org/10.1037/0003-066X.54.7.493

11 Abigail Paterson, et al., 'Evidence that implementation intentions reduce self-harm in the community', British Journal of Health Psychology, 2023 https://bpspsychub.onlinelibrary.wiley.com/doi/10.1111/bjhp.12682

12 'Executive Assistant Demographics and Statistics in the US', Zippia https://www.zippia.com/executive-assistant-jobs/demographics/

13 'The Definitive 100 Most Useful Productivity Tips', Filtered https://learn.filtered.com/hubfs/Definitive%20100%20Most%20Useful%20Productivity%20Hacks.pdf

14 Echoes of George Berkeley's 300-year-old, still-unanswered, question, 'If a tree falls in a forest and no one is around to hear it, does it make a sound?'

15   'How can you make time last longer?', *Radio 4 in Four*, BBC Sounds https://www.bbc.co.uk/sounds/play/p041vcb6

16   https://www.youtube.com/watch?v=ideZXg-TLz8

17   Timeboxing can very easily stretch to include various forms of journaling by utilizing the Notes field, for example.

18   'Mental Health at Work', World Health Organisation, 2022 https://www.who.int/news-room/fact-sheets/detail/mental-health-at-work

19   Nader Hajloo, 'Relationships Between Self-Efficacy, Self-Esteem and Procrastination in Undergraduate Psychology Students', *IJPBS*, 2014 https://www.ncbi.nlm.nih.gov/pmc/articles/PMC4359724/

20   Brad Aeon, et al., 'Does Time-Management Work? A Meta-Analysis', PLoS One, 2021 https://www.ncbi.nlm.nih.gov/pmc/articles/PMC7799745/

21   Nick Fitz, 'Batching Smartphone Notifications Can Improve Well-Being', Computers in Human Behaviour, 2019 https://www.academia.edu/36928325/Batching_smartphone_notifications_can_improve_well_being

22   www.theguardian.com/on-my-terms/2022/sep/01/its-past-your-worry-time-four-ways-to-stop-overthinking-and-enjoy-yourself

23   Leonie C. Steckermeier, 'The Value of Autonomy for the Good Life. An Empirical Investigation of Autonomy and Life Satisfaction in Europe', Soc Indic Res, 2021 https://link.springer.com/article/10.1007/s11205-020-02565-8

24   https://www.instagram.com/reel/Cnitexrhs7K/?igshid=YmMyMTA2M2Y%3D

25   Ray A. Smith, 'Workers Now Spend Two Full Days a Week on Email and in Meetings', *The Wall Street Journal*, 2023 https://www.wsj.com/articles/workers-say-its-harder-to-get-things-done-now-heres-why-2a5f1389

26   Daniel J Levitin, 'Why the Modern World is Bad For Your Brain', *Guardian*, 2015 www.theguardian.com/science/2015/jan/18/modern-world-bad-for-brain-daniel-j-levitin-organized-mind-information-overload

27   https://ecal.com/70-percent-of-adults-rely-on-digital-calendar/

28   Peter F. Drucker, 'What Makes an Effective Executive', Harvard Business Review, 2004 https://hbr.org/2004/06/what-makes-an-effective-executive

29   Cal Newport calls out misinterpretations of Parkinson's 1955 paper, but I will focus on the famous misquote, which has captured the imagination for the last 70 years. https://www.calnewport.com/blog/2008/06/11/debunking-parkinsons-law/

30   Laura A. Brannon, et al., 'Timeless Demonstrations of Parkinson's First Law', Psychonomic Bulletin & Review, 1999 https://www.researchgate.net/publication/11189704_Timeless_demonstrations_of_Parkinson's_first_law

31   Elliot Aronson, et al., 'Further Steps Beyond Parkinson's Law', Journal of Experimental Social Psychology, 1967 https://www.sciencedirect.com/science/article/abs/pii/0022103167900297

32   Dianna M. Tice, et al., 'Longitudinal Study of Procrastination, Performance, Stress, and Health', Psychological Science, 1997 https://psycnet.apa.org/record/1997-43695-008

33   Maria De Paola, Francesca Gioia, 'Who Performs Better Under Time Pressure?', IZA, 2014 https://docs.iza.org/dp8708.pdf

34   American Psychological Association, 'Multitasking: Switching Costs', 2006 https://www.apa.org/topics/research/multitasking

35   https://www.nhtsa.gov/risky-driving/distracted-driving

36   Katharina Buchholz, 'Which Countries Spend the Most Time on Social Media?' World Economic Forum, 2022 https://www.weforum.org/agenda/2022/04/social-media-internet-connectivity/

37   https://markmanson.net/are-you-not-entertained

38   https://www.eurekalert.org/news-releases/883606

39   Marc Zao-Sanders, 'How Timeboxing Works and Why It Will Make You More Productive', Harvard Business Review, 2018 https://hbr.org/2018/12/how-timeboxing-works-and-why-it-will-make-you-more-productive

40   Blue, apparently, boosts creativity: 'Effect of Colours: Blue Boosts Creativity', University of British Columbia, 2009 https://www.sciencedaily.com/releases/2009/02/090205142143.htm#:~:text=Effect%20Of%20Colors%3A%20Blue%20Boosts,Attention%20To%20Detail%20%2D%2D%20ScienceDaily

41   'What Are Your Chances of Living to 100?', Office for National Statistics, 2016 https://www.ons.gov.uk/peoplepopulationandcommunity/birthsdeathsandmarriages/lifeexpectancies/articles/whatareyourchancesoflivingto100/2016-01-14

42   Rachel Gillett, 'People over 65 shared their greatest regret in life', Independent, 2016 https://www.independent.co.uk/life-style/health-and-families/features/people-over-65-shared-their-greatest-regret-in-life-the-most-common-one-may-surprise-you-a6800851.html

43   Sarah Crow, Dana Schulz, '50 Regrets Everyone Has Over 50', BestLife, 2023 https://bestlifeonline.com/most-common-regrets/

44   A. Pawlowski, 'How to live life without major regrets', Today, 2017 https://www.today.com/health/biggest-regrets-older-people-share-what-they-d-do-differently-t118918

45   https://www.independent.co.uk/life-style/health-and-families/features/people-over-65-shared-their-greatest-regret-in-life-the-most-common-one-may-surprise-you-a6800851.html

46   https://news.microsoft.com/2008/01/14/survey-shows-increasing-worldwide-reliance-on-to-do-lists/

47   Janet Choi, 'How to Master the Art of To-Do Lists by Understanding Why they Fail', IDoneThis, 2021 http://blog.idonethis.com/how-to-master-the-art-of-to-do-lists/

48 Corinne Purtill, 'The New Science of Forgetting', Time, 2022 https://time.com/6171190/new-science-of-forgetting/

49 https://www.campaignmonitor.com/resources/knowledge-base/how-many-emails-does-the-average-person-receive-per-day/

50 https://www.newswiretoday.com/news/76151/New-Survey-Reveals-Average-Brit-Has-27-Conversations-Every-Day/

51 Daniel Kahneman, 'Intuitive Prediction: Biases and Corrective Procedures', Advanced Decision Technology Program, 1977 https://apps.dtic.mil/dtic/tr/fulltext/u2/a047747.pdf

52 Britain's famous, timeboxing chef: https://www.jamieoliver.com/recipes/category/books/jamies-30-minute-meals/

53 'Why You Should Skip the Easy Wins and Tackle the Hard Task First', KelloggInsight, 2019 https://insight.kellogg.northwestern.edu/article/easy-or-hard-tasks-first

54 Mark Lieber, 'Night Owls Have 10% Higher Mortality Risk', CNN Health, 2018 https://edition.cnn.com/2018/04/12/health/night-owl-mortality-risk-study/index.html

55 Carolyn Schur, 'Night Owls', Alert@Work, 2023 https://alertatwork.com/percentage-of-night-owls-early-birds-and-intermediates-in-the-general-population

56 Courtney Connley, 'The simple trick Steve Jobs followed to be "most productive"', CNBC Make It, 2021 https://www.cnbc.com/2021/05/27/steve-jobs-former-assistant-on-what-he-did-to-be-most-productive.html

57 Mo Selim: https://vimeo.com/226508728

58 Voltaire, *La Bégueule*, 1772

59 Joseph F. Ferrari, et al., 'Procrastination', Encyclopedia of Personality and Individual Differences. Springer, Cham., 2020 https://link.springer.com/referenceworkentry/10.1007/978-3-319-24612-3_2272

60 Psychological Bulletin, Vol. 133, No. 1

61 See page 295

62 https://www.youtube.com/watch?v=vJG698U2Mvo

63 Eric H Schumacher, et al., 'Virtually Perfect Time Sharing in Dual-Task Performance', Psychological Science, 2001 https://journals.sagepub.com/doi/pdf/10.1111/1467-9280.00318

64 Kelvin F. H. Lui, et al., 'Does Media Multitasking Always Hurt? Psychon Bull Rev, 2012 https://pubmed.ncbi.nlm.nih.gov/22528869/

65 James Clear, 'How to Build New Habits by Taking Advantage of Old Ones', Habit Stacking (https://jamesclear.com/habit-stacking#) where Clear credits Fogg for the idea

66 Sam Harris, 'Death and the Present Moment', speech at the Global Atheist Convention, April 2012

67 'Research Proves Your Brain Needs Breaks', Work Trend Index, Microsoft, 2021 https://www.microsoft.com/en-us/worklab/work-trend-index/brain-research

68 Immanuel Kant, the philosopher, was a fan of these.

69 This might be a visualization, breathing exercises, revising your notes, rehearsing, positive affirmation.

70 R. J. Kaplan, et al., 'Dietry protein, carbohydrate and fat enhance memory performance in healthy elderly', Am J Clin Nutr, 2001 https://pubmed.ncbi.nlm.nih.gov/11684539/

71 Derek Thompson, 'A Formula for Perfect Productivity', *The Atlantic*, 2014 https://www.theatlantic.com/business/archive/2014/09/science-tells-you-how-many-minutes-should-you-take-a-break-for-work-17/380369/

72 Christiano R. R. Alves, et al., 'Influence of Acute High-Intensity Aerobic Interval Exercise Bout on Selective Attention and Short-Term Memory Tasks', Perceptual and Motor Skills, 2014 https://journals.sagepub.com/doi/abs/10.2466/22.06.PMS.118k10w4

73 'Brief Diversions Vastly Improve Focus', Science Daily, 2011 https://www.sciencedaily.com/releases/2011/02/110208131529.htm

74 Leah A. Irish, et al., 'The role of sleep hygiene in promoting public health: A review of empirical evidence', Sleep Medicine Reviews, 2015 https://www.sciencedirect.com/science/article/abs/pii/S1087079214001002?via%3Dihub

75 If you're interested in the history and science behind these assumptions, I recommend Matthew Walker's *Why We Sleep* or Russell Foster's *Life Time*.

76 Mohamed Boubekri, et al., 'Impact of Windows and Daylight Exposure on Overall Health and Sleep Quality of Office Workers', JCSM, 2014 https://jcsm.aasm.org/doi/10.5664/jcsm.3780

77 Fahdah A. Alshobaili, et al., 'The effect of smartphone usage at bedtime on sleep quality among Saudi non-medical staff at King Saud University Medical City', JFMPC, 2019 https://www.ncbi.nlm.nih.gov/pmc/articles/PMC6618184

78 A simple definition of technology is: the application of knowledge for practical purposes.

79 Cassie Shortsleeve, 'A Guide to Doing Nothing for People Who Are Really Bad At It', Self, 2022 https://www.self.com/story/guide-to-doing-nothing

80 Krystal Hu, 'ChatGPT sets record', Reuters, 2023 https://www.reuters.com/technology/chatgpt-sets-record-fastest-growing-user-base-analyst-note-2023-02-01/

81 Marc Zao-Sanders, 'The most frequently used English noun', One Thing at a Time, 2023 https://marczaosanders.substack.com/p/the-most-frequently-used-english